On and Off th

THE LIFE OF A
WESTMORLAND RAILWAYMAN

~

Len Clark

Best Wishes
Len Clark.

HELM
PRESS

Dedicated to my wife, Dorothy and family

Published by Helm Press

10 Abbey Gardens, Natland, Kendal, Cumbria LA9 7SP

Tel: 015395 61321

Copyright – Len Clark 2003

First published October 2003

Typeset in

ISBN 0 9540497 4 8

Typeset and printed by Miller Turner Printers, The Sidings, Beezon

Fields, Kendal, Cumbria LA9 6BL

Front cover: Derailment at Grayrigg 1966, Paul Allonby

Back cover:

CONTENTS

Tebay Station 1900 – LNWR. It had its own gashouse (shown in the centre of the picture) behind the Loco Shed which provided lighting for the shed, platform, terraces and church.

John Marsh Photo Archive

Introduction

I was born the son of a railwayman and brought up in and around the village of Tebay, which was known as a railway village as so many people worked there. So it is hardly surprising that for as long as I can remember all I ever wanted to do was to work on the railways.

My Grandma and Auntie Janie helped dad to bring me, my brother and sister up after my mother died when I was only six. They brought us up well; they had been farmers and still kept hens, ducks and a pig. Dad was a keen fisherman and by an early age I could fish both legally and illegally. I did well at primary school, passed the Eleven Plus and went to Kendal Grammar School but nevertheless one of my happiest days was when I left school just short of my fifteenth birthday.

I did farm work until I was old enough to get work on the railways. My first job was as a junior porter at Low Gill. I used to get the train one direction and pushbike the other along the 'cess'.

After this I got a job as an engine cleaner in the Tebay Loco Sheds and passed out as a fireman cleaner. Then I did two years National Service and went into the Army Catering Corps. I returned to the Loco Sheds and after a short time was made redundant. Got myself a job driving a wagon until an opening came up on the Permanent Way. I remained there until I retired after 46 years service in February 2001.

I look back on these days as if they were yesterday with these wonderful steam trains, banking engines going up Shap summit, with my many mates, the work, comradeship and jokes we played. It was hard work but fun at the same time, if there was a spare five minutes at dinner time and we were near a beck, we would be trying to nab trout and were usually successful and if there were rabbits, I would bring a ferret next day and put it down the hole.

I wanted to write about my life and last winter I did just that. I would like to thank particularly John Marsh and Jay Hartley for all their photographs they contributed and Anne Bonney for compiling. I have made it as accurate as I can remember and acknowledged the use of people's photographs.

All this could never have been done or achieved without my wife Dorothy whom I would like to thank, who never complained once about me going out at all times of day and night for work in all those years. All it remains for me now to say is, read on and enjoy 'On and off the Rails!'

Len Clark
August 2003

1

Family and School Days

I was born on the 30 July 1937, the eldest son of a Tebay railwayman and was given the name Leonard William Clark. I lived with my dad, mum, brother and sister at No. 1 Borrow Bridge Cottages only yards from the London North Western Railway, nowadays called the West Coast Main Line. There were three cottages altogether and they lay about a mile and a half south of Tebay, between the West Coast Main Line and the main Appleby to Kendal road. These cottages were later demolished before the M6 motorway was built in 1967.

My dad was also called Leonard and was the eldest son of Jack Clark, the local policeman from Shap. My mother was Rene (Irene) Sergeant, daughter of Hannah Sergeant and William who used to farm at Roundthwaite Farm, in Roundthwaite, and was one of a large family.

I was the oldest, then two years later my brother Raymond was born, and two years after him my sister, Marion. All his life dad was called Len and I have been likewise. He was born at Milnthorpe, he was a signalman on the railway and worked between Scout Green and Lambrigg. Before he married he had been a gamekeeper and was always very keen on shooting, fishing, trapping and such like.

Mam came from Roundthwaite, a small hamlet with six farms and six cottages, and that is where I was born. In those days it was the norm for women to give birth at home. Today there are only two farms left, the rest have been converted into houses and holiday homes.

Dad was a keen gardener and had a large vegetable and flower garden and grew potatoes, cabbage, carrots and Brussel sprouts together with sweet peas, chrysants and dahlias. He also had a big greenhouse and grew tomatoes and lettuce.

Tebay lies at the head of the Lune valley, with the Howgills lying to the east and Shap Fells to the west. The famous Shap Bank starts from Tebay and has a gradient of 1 in 75 and is five and a half miles long. Tebay gets a large amount of rainfall as it is surrounded by hills. An old chap once

Dad and mum on their wedding day standing outside Roundthwaite Farm with cousin Shelia Sergeant as bridesmaid. Behind is Billy Clark (left) and Jack Parsley. *late Madge Sergeant*

The three of us, Marion aged 6, Raymond aged 8 and me aged 10. *Taylor's Photo Studio, Morecambe*

told me, 'If you can see them hills it's going to rain, if you can't its raining!'

When I was only six years old, tragedy struck our family. My mother took ill with pneumonia, which was a serious complaint in those days and she had to go to hospital at Carlisle. There was the three of us at home and dad was working shifts. By that time I had started school at Tebay Infants and I used to walk the one and half miles to school. There were very few cars on the road then. Up to the age of eleven, I always wore clogs, short corduroy pants, jacket, socks my grandma had knitted and a cap.

I had to take my lunch with me as there was no canteen then and had a few sandwiches and a bit of cake Auntie Janie had made. Everyone used to get a small bottle of milk to drink at morning break. My teacher was Mrs Moss and her family still live in Tebay today. Dad took my brother and sister to stay at grandma's and Auntie Janie's at Beckside, Roundthwaite. Janie was my mam's sister and she never married but looked after my grandma and later us.

I went to Shap to stay with my other grandma and Granddad Clark. I did not want to leave my brother and sister but dad made me go. My granddad as I said was the policeman at Shap and he was very well liked in the village. He lived opposite the Police Station and after he retired he lived at Brook House, at the north end of the village. I remember him in his tunic, with his whistle and baton. A quiet, sociable man, who looked something like Jack Warner, who used to play the policeman called, Dixon, in 'Dixon of Dock Green' that was on television in the 1960s.

When farmers dipped their sheep in those days the local policeman had to go and watch that it was carried out properly and he used to take me with him. Dad used to come to Shap every night to see me and grandma and granddad. In their conversation they never ever mentioned mam when I was there.

I remember dad came home this night and I thought something strange was going on because they had been talking about mam and when I came into the room everybody went quiet. Then a week or so later he came and said I could come back to grandma's at Beckside Cottage and be with my brother and sister again. This was what I had been waiting for but only to find out, that my mam was no longer with us and had sadly died leaving us all behind.

Most nights dad went to Borrow Bridge to put a good fire on and I had to go with him to the empty house. One good thing was we never had to buy coal living next to the railway line, as the local firemen always used to

My mum aged 12, Auntie Janie and
Auntie Alice Parsley

Herbert, Lancaster

Roundthwaite, Tebay, in the early 1900s.

Raphael Tuck & Sons Ltd/John Marsh Photo Archive

kick a cob or two off. Yorkshire coal was the best but of course it was meant for steam engines and got very hot and we went through a lot of grate bottoms! I suppose dad didn't mind as he was getting it for now't!

We were all staying now at Beckside Cottage and rightly named as the beck ran close by. It was a very old house, which must have been a farm at one time as it had a barn with a sink mew on each side. A sink mew is where the hay went and with a byre underneath. Grandma used to keep coal and wood in the sink mew and hen food in the byre. By the time I was born Granddad Sergeant had died and grandma had given up farming and moved into Beckside. Grandma's maiden name was Whitehead.

After a short time dad advertised for a housekeeper and a lady came to see him. He must have thought she was all right because it was back to Borrow Bridge for us. I think I gave her a hell of a life, as she went after two or three weeks and we got another one. She could not make anything of me and I just would not settle, all I wanted to do was to be back with grandma and Auntie Janie.

Auntie Janie used to work in the Refreshment Room on Tebay Station, which was a very busy place in the 1940s and 50s. You could get tea, coffee, beer, sandwiches, cakes etc. During the war Auntie Janie used to bring us crisps and the occasional banana, as things were bad to get hold of then.

Things got that bad at home that during the school holidays when dad was working night duty and weekends he would take me with him. This particular time he was on nights at Scout Green Box and I went with him sitting on the cross bar of his bike. Scout Green was situated in one of the most remote places on the West Coast Main Line, three miles north of Tebay and mid way up Shap Bank. When modification came, this box was taken down and sent to a private railway in Sittingbourne, Kent. In the signal box there were three wooden boxes all in a row and I used to sleep on them. These boxes were where the signalmen kept their slippers, cups, frying pan, plates etc. Dad often used to take some bacon and eggs and have a fry up. These signal boxes always had a good fire and some times an oven as well. The railwaymen often took drinking water with them if there was no spring nearby. Scout Green was only a very small box with six or seven levers and one of these was for the road crossing gates. The road was only used two or three times a day, mainly by farmers, though it was also a well-known place for train spotters and people with cameras. In the summer time you could hear the lovely sound of the curlew, pee-wit (lapwing) and skylark together with the occasional ba from sheep grazing nearby.

11

I remember during that summer, one particular Friday afternoon I took it into my head that I was not going back to Borrow Bridge as I should of done but instead went to Beckside, which was about a mile to the west of Tebay. When I got there the door was wide open, as you could leave it safely in them days. There was nobody in, I shouted but got no reply. I then went and hid under the stairs and all I could hear was the grandfather clock chiming every hour. I sat there in total darkness. I heard Grandma and Aunt Janie come in and get their tea, clear away and wash up. Afterwards they went out the back into their big garden. Then after a while, that seemed like a week to me, I heard dad come into the house with them and ask if they had seen me? Of course the answer was, 'No,' I then heard the clock strike six. There was a search party out for me, including the local police. The village bobby at that time was PC McCracken. Seven o'clock struck and I thought it was time I broke cover. I was by now, cold, hungry and in need of the toilet. Expecting a good hiding, I was wrong, grandma hugged me in total relief and I started to cry. She made me something to eat and I gratefully stayed the night.

Next day dad came for me but I was not for going and created a hell of a carry on. Grandma said to him, 'It's going to be no good, let him come and live with us?' So this he did agree to. This was just what I wanted and it was going to be the start of a new life. There was no electricity or hot water. We had an Aladdin paraffin lamp, candles and little Kelly lamps that we took to our bedrooms. I had to get used to no trains roaring past but a beck instead that I started fishing happily in.

The comics I used to read in those days were the Beano, Dandy and a little later the Eagle. As time went on I got jobs to do, as grandma had plenty on her plate with us three and dad. She kept about forty hens, they were Black Leghorn crossed with Rhode Island Red, a good laying strain. She also had some ducks and a pig. When we killed the pig there would be a lot of work. First it would be cut up and pieces would be cured in salt and salt petre and then hung from the beam on hooks in the living room. Aunt Alice Parsley (a neighbour) and Auntie Janie used to make sausages and black pudding (oatmeal and blood) from it and best of all from our point of view was when they used to dry the pig's bladder and we would blow it up and play football with it.

As soon as Aunt Janie came home from work she was straight into the housework and had set days for the numerous jobs. Monday was always washday; Tuesday ironing; Wednesday baking; Thursday cleaning bedrooms and Friday for downstairs and of course none of today's labour saving devices. Auntie Janie used a dolly tub to wash the clothes; this was

Grandma (Sarah) and Granddad (Billy) Sergeant outside Roundthwaite Farm, looking across to Tebay Fell in the 1930s. *late Madge Sergeant*

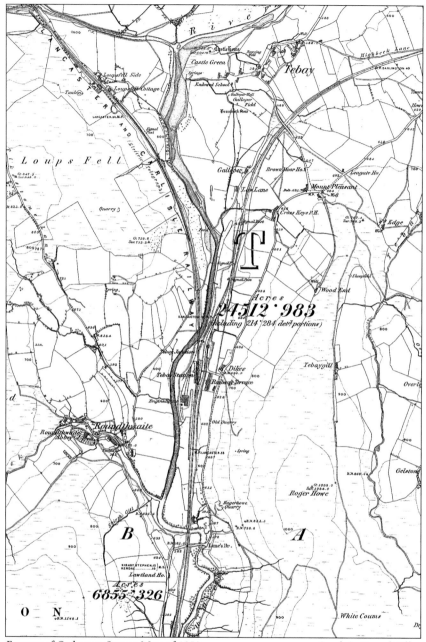

Excerpt of Ordnance Survey Map of 1858.   *Cumbria Record Office*

a round zinc tub about three feet high. Then dolly legs were used. These had four wooden legs attached to the bottom of a shaft like a spade and a handle across the top and you twisted it left to right to wash the clothes. She also had a mangle, which had two heavy rollers set on legs that revolved closely together when you turned the wheel and the clothes would pass between and the excess water would be squeezed out. After the washing was hung out to dry the final job would be the ironing the following day. The steel iron would be warmed in front of the fire. A very tiring job altogether.

My job on a Thursday night was to do the eggs and box them up ready for collection next day. The Express Dairy from Appleby came round with the egg wagon. Saturday mornings I used to walk to Tebay Station to collect the papers from the Book Stall where Elsie Preston (husband a railwayman) worked. That suited me as I stayed till dinnertime collecting train numbers that I had done since I was knee high. Railways were in my blood, I couldn't help it. All I ever wanted to do when I left school was to work on those steam trains. Another little job I sometimes did was taking the wet battery off the wireless to Doug Major's shop to be charged up. His shop was called 'Little Woolworths.' You could buy anything there from a safety pin to a new bike. The biggest fault was he never knew where anything was. What a scrow it was! He had a brother called Ernie, who was a cobbler and was kept busy repairing footwear. Apart from his shop, Doug was also the postman and went round on a pushbike. One day on my way to Doug's shop, I was passing the Institute and was just opposite John Rae's joiners shop. He was just going in and I asked him what he was doing? His reply was, 'Oh I's guy busy today, come in and see.' So I did. He was making a coffin. I stayed and watched him for a while.

During the severe winter of 1946–47 I walked to school from Roundthwaite, only missing one day. The lane was blocked solid for weeks on end. I walked at wall top height and as I said, we used to wear clogs and short corduroy pants, so you can imagine. My aunt did all the mending, she was a good hand at sewing, darning and knitting. At about the age of eight we left the infants school and went to the top of the village to the senior school. In these days there would be about thirty children in the infants and about sixty in seniors. There were three classrooms. My first teacher was Mary Rae and didn't she know how to use a ruler. Not on paper but to give it to you across the hand, edgeways on. The headmaster then was Danny Robinson and if he met you in the village and you did not courteously lift your cap and say, 'Good after-

noon Sir or Good evening Sir!' Then you could be sure the cane was waiting for you next day.

At school we used to play all the usual games in them days, marbles,
conkers – these we used to get off chestnut trees in the autumn and bore
a hole through the centre and thread some string through. One of you
held the conker up, while the other hit it and you took it in turns. The
one that smashed up first had lost. Quoits, these were a round piece of
metal that we used to throw to a peg in the ground about fifteen yards
away. We also of course played football. One day I was playing football
with my brother, Raymond, Nathan and Brian Guy. Nat Guy farmed at
Town Head, Roundthwaite and we went to school with these lads. They
had a dog that always showed its teeth at you and if you were on your
bike it would sneak up behind and bite the back tyre. This day it grabbed
my backside and tore a hole in my pants leaving big tooth marks. My old
friend, Tom Richardson from Orton said to me, 'Never trust a grinning
dog.' How right he is!

On Saturday afternoons I had to clean the hens out, two big huts.
Make sure they had plenty of clean straw in the nest boxes and chopped
straw on the floor for them to scratch among. Dad was far more settled
by this time and we were one big happy family. Quite often during the
holidays I used to go on the 9am train to Carlisle Citadel Station to collect train numbers. Carlisle was a very busy place. Trains from Edinburgh
and Newcastle came in with a North Eastern engine on. I would usually
get back to Tebay at 3pm.

Dad was a very keen fisherman and a founder member of Tebay
Fishing Club. It was formed in 1944 by a dozen local railwaymen, who
used to raffle a packet of cigarettes in the Junction Hotel every Saturday
night. The River Lune is one of the best salmon and trout-rivers in the
North of England today. Dad taught me how to fish, always wanting me
to go with him to hold the net. He also could catch them illegally using
the 'Tebay Fly' as it was called then, or a lamp and gaff used during the
hours of darkness. The Tebay Fly was illegally fishing with rod and line
commonly known as 'snatching'. When the salmon came up the river
towards autumn the Tebay Fly came into use. It consisted of a large treble
hook on the end of a wire trace, then a bead threaded on followed by an
artificial minnow made from lead. Dad had a mould to make these with;
he knew where the favourite places were, for salmon lying. It was the sink
and draw method, totally forbidden these days. My job was always to

Facing page: Scout Green in 1965 with the Jubilee Class No. 45586 on its way to
Carlisle. Note the jointed track and telegraph poles – all now gone. *N. Stead/author's*

watch for the water bailiff arriving, as most of the salmon were not hooked by the mouth and by law, had to be returned to the water. Most people caught salmon with this method until 1966 when a terrible disease came along in the autumn of 1967 called, Ulcerative Dermal Necrosis (U.D.N.) and the fish became covered in large scabs and died.

One favourite place for fishermen was the Old Lune's Bridge, south of Tebay, where the river rushed down the narrow rock stretch, different parts of it had names like The Pinnacle, The Flat, The Ginnal, Rock Side, Top Hole and Bottom Hole. Salmon rested in these places before tackling the very rough water ahead and they had to jump to get up. This area is now out of bounds during September and October. During the late 1940s Tebay had no less than a dozen shops, Mrs Bamber had two grocers shops, one at either end of the village. She was a big Chapel person but if dad sent me for some tobacco on a Sunday morning she always obliged. Grandma was also a Methodist and I had to go to Sunday school every week without fail and I was a member of the choir, as I always loved singing. In February 1952 I was awarded a Philip Lord Wharton Bible.

My Uncle Nat (mam's brother) and Auntie Madge lived only two hundred yards from us, at Roundthwaite. They had a daughter called Sheila who now lives at Warton, near Carnforth, with husband Ronnie. Uncle Nat was a guard on the railway and also keen on fishing. One day I was walking back home from a fishing session with dad along Roundthwaite Beck when we saw two big salmon. He made right for Uncle Nat's and told him what he had seen, a cock and hen (male and female). He said, 'We will go at 7pm and get the cock fish as the hen would nobat (only) be full of eggs.' Nat said, 'I, o'rite.' At 7pm dad was getting the lamp and gaff out and I told him I wanted to go as well but he told me I would have to stay with Auntie Madge, which reluctantly I did. Within fifteen minutes they were back in the house with a seventeen-pound cock fish. I had learned one thing about poaching at an early stage, never go looking for fish with a lamp in the dark unless you know exactly where they are, otherwise you will get caught. I stood and watched them gut it and steak it up, thinking it wouldn't be long before I was doing that sort of thing myself.

Auntie Madge said to dad, 'Len Clark you are showing your son bad habits,' he smiled and said, 'Ay well, he'll niver lam (learn) younger!' Auntie Madge used to go to Greenholme once a week to clean up for a farmer called Billy Wilson. She also made butter sometimes and I would go and turn the churn handle for her.

Tebay Senior School in 1900 – at the top end of the village. Now a Youth Hostel.
John Marsh Photo Archive

Early 1900s picture of Tebay Station. The Refreshment Room where Auntie Janie worked was in the centre of the southbound platform. Overhead walkway can be seen in the centre. *John Marsh Photo Archive*

Tebay in the 1940s with the Junction Hotel on the right and Doug Majors shop to the left of it and two rows of railway houses. Also in left hand corner is the Co-op which is now the Barnaby Rudge Tavern.

Mountain View, Tebay and on the left can be seen Mrs Bamber's grocers shop.
The R.A.P. Co Ltd, London/John Marsh Photo Archive

A farmer just up the road from us at Roundthwaite Abbey, was called Billy Parsley and we used to call his wife Auntie Alice as she was very good to us. They had a son called Jack whom I got friendly with, as I used to go and help at hay time and catch sheep at dipping time. On winter's nights I used to go and see them quite often, we played darts, which he taught me to play. They used to collect peat from a big bog and stand it out till it was dry then I helped to bring it in with horse and sledge. You could smell it burning on the fire a hundred yards away. One night I went up to the Abbey when they were having their supper, they all had a trout on the plate. I knew Jack was no fisherman but soon found out how he had got them, the same method as dad and Uncle Nat. If you went in their house while the Archers were on the radio you were not allowed to speak, as Billy always listened to it.

Billy had a brother Jim living with them, he was very lame. Besides Jack they had two daughters, Norah and Mabel, neither of them married. Mabel, who is no longer with us, was a nurse at Lancaster, while Nora worked at Abbey Farm and still lives in Roundthwaite. Jack married a girl called Ruth, from Kendal, and they have two daughters, Linda and Jacqueline and a son, Michael, who all live in Roundthwaite.

During haytime Jack would go and mow with the horses getting up around 4.30am while the dew was still on the grass and before the heat of the day came, as the horse didn't like clegs (big flies that stung). After milking Bill and Jim would follow on, to do a bit of hacking with the scythe (hacking is round the field edge and in the corners). Today they just let the cows in after the hay is picked up and they clean all the grass up that wasn't cut. Jim's job was mainly on the cart taking hay off the forkers.

Just opposite Jack's house was a waterfall where fish had to jump to get up and there was a natural hollow in the rock about two feet long by four inches wide caused from hundreds of years of wear. We used to place a round stone at the low end, so when fish jumped into it they had no escape; we called it the 'trap'. This was looked at two or three times a day, we have had many a good feed out of the trap.

I first learned to milk a cow at the Abbey, it was a Shorthorn with long teats, and very quiet, it let its milk down easily. Some cows were hard to milk especially if it was a heifer (a cow having had its first calf). They used to stamp about and sometimes kick. There were only two or three paraffin lamps that lit the cow shed during winter, so you were almost in darkness.

Loading hay in 1948 with new Ferguson tractor is Billy Parsley, Jim Parsley on the hay and Nora and Jack.

Nora Parsley

Teatime in the hayfield in 1958. Nora, Billy, Auntie Alice and a friend, with Jim Parsley sitting on the cart.

Nora Parsley

An early 1900s picture of Roundthwaite Abbey, Tebay – home of the Parsley family.
Town Head Farm on the right was home to the Guy family.   *C Lowis, Tebay*

Just across from the Abbey was another farm called Town View. The farmer's name was Bill Hunter. He was a bit of a character, I was walking through his yard one day and he was just coming out of the house, he said to me, "Now mi lad how 'ister?" (how are you). I said, "Alright thank you." His reply was,"Oh well be thankful thou is!" What a true saying that is. His grandson Geoff and granddaughter Margaret live only a few doors away from us in Tebay.

Apart from fishing and shooting we always kept a ferret. A good time to go ferreting was when the snow was lying, you could see which holes were being used, saving a lot of time, they seemed to bolt well on the snow, also when it had been hard frost. We mostly kept a gill (female) ferret but the only trouble was when they came on heat (ready for mating) you had to get them mated, otherwise you could lose them.

One day during October I thought dad would be going fishing onto 'The Flat' as the water was just at the right height, as it had to be. I went on my bike and of course acted as 'look out' man. I had an old Raleigh with high handlebars. I stood on the bridge with my cap on and if I took it off, they understood the bailiff had come on the scene. Dad was standing next to Harvey Preston. He was a railwayman on the Permanent Way, later on becoming my ganger. He lived on Whinfell Terrace with his wife, Elsie, who as I said worked in the bookstall on Tebay Station. Harvey was a good footballer in his younger days.

It wasn't long before he had two very big salmon out. He told me to take them home on my bike. I fastened some thin rope through their gills and tied them onto the handlebars, one on either side. Their tails were touching the ground. When I got home I weighed them, one was nineteen and the other was twenty-two pounds. If a salmon was a bit dark in colour, as they could be late on in the season (after they had been in fresh water for some time, as Tebay was about thirty-seven miles from the Lune Estuary), we used to wrap them in a wet cloth and that made them look better. Today all dark coloured fish must be put back into the river unharmed. Dad along with many other people used to make their tobacco money by selling salmon. Visitors, who came to stay at the Junction Hotel, always wanted two or three to take home.

Friday night was bath night; we all took our turns, my brother and sister, then me. We had a long tin bath in front of the fire; the fireplace had a water tank on one side, a crane that we hung the kettle on and an oven that we used for baking in. During winter nights Aunt Janie used to make peg rugs. I used to cut old jackets and pants up for her to use. She had a wooden frame, stretched hessian bags across and these formed the underside and backing to the rug. The pieces of material were then pulled through and threaded tightly together to form a sort of pile. The hessian bags had contained farm feeding stuff, hen food and such like. Nothing was ever wasted in them days – they knew all about recycling they had

Dad in No 1 Box at Tebay showing the levers and instruments above. Dad was 6' 5" tall and was nicknamed 'Tiny'!

The old railway bridge that crossed the River Lune at Blamire's Pool in 1948 showing the plate layers cabin on the left. The bridge was renewed in 1983. The M6 motorway is only a short distance away and runs parallel with it.

nothing to learn. Sometimes she made rugs with wool using the same idea. Grandma would always be knitting socks or jumpers for us.

Although Tebay was a thriving village with a dozen shops they are now long gone. Harold Stainton used to come round taking orders for coal and groceries from the Co-op. Tebay had two Co-ops then. The one at the south end sold groceries, vegetables and paraffin. The one at the north end of the village was a drapers shop. We also dealt with Thomas Dixon and Son, from Ravenstonedale, who brought our hen feed and pig meal. Jack Smith used to come round for the orders and later it was Alex Greenlees. I always sat and listened to the crack and found it interesting. You hardly had to go away for shopping. The fish van came round once a week, a little man, Walter Wood who always wore a trilby and later worked in Bill McClure's shop in Kendal. There were buses, the school bus and maybe a couple in between. Everybody helped one another in these days, you looked in on your neighbours if they were ill and helped with shopping.

We also had Charlie Bell the baker who came round in an old van, likewise Hilton Coats the Butcher in his old Morris van. Charlie used to go round the outlying houses and hamlets reaching us about 3pm on his way back to Kendal and by that time he had nearly always sold out. Hilton Coats was always smartly dressed wearing black leather leggings and black boots that were always highly polished. He used to give us sweets. He lived at Orton. The Co-op at the station end of the village was very busy. It is now the Barnaby Rudge Tavern. Walter Askew was manager, along with Harold Stainton, Nellie Nevison and Doris Metcalfe.

Uncle Nat and Auntie Madge Sergeant moved to Carnforth, to live at 55 Grosvenor Place, when Nat became a passenger guard doing double trip runs to London. Booking off, he would stay overnight in the railway hostel, then worked back next day.

When children reached the age of eleven you had to sit a stiff exam called the 'Eleven Plus'. This I did and passed, I don't know how because I wasn't that brainy. I went to Kendal Grammar School. I hated it from the first day to my last. It cost dad a fortune getting me rigged up with uniform, green blazer with badge, grey pants, socks etc. Aunt Janie had to put a nametag in each item. It was a long day, walking half-a-mile to catch the Ribble Bus in all weathers, sometimes wet through before getting on the bus. The twelve-mile trip to Kendal, New Road, then another half-mile walk to school, at the very south end of town, it was a nine and a half hour day, plus homework every night. At Kendal we played rugby in winter and cricket in summer. The school also had its own gym and swimming baths.

Dad sometimes shot a hare and I had to take it to Bowman's Game Shop, in Kendal, before going to school and he got two shillings each for them. Our rabbits went to McClure's. Bowman's shop was in Stramongate near the Dun Horse Pub. They used to have hares, rabbits, ducks and pheasants hanging up outside the door and also sold fruit and vegetables. Bill McClure's shop was on Highgate, below the Town Hall. Bill was a keen hound trailing man and now lives in Windermere. I also used to pick rosehips when they were ripe and take them to a place in Lowther Street, usually a pillowcase full at a time for a bit of pocket money.

The only good thing about going to Kendal, was I saw the eight twenty-nine passenger train stood in Kendal Station every morning. I caught the number, it used to have a Scot or Jubilee on. One day the

Facing page: En route for Stainmore leaving Tebay on the N.E. line is a BR 2-6-0 built at Swindon in 1954 (double-headed). First engine is No. 77003.

N. Stead Collection/John Marsh Photo Archive

An early 1900s picture of the iron bridge that crosses over the River Lune at Low Lane. This is the main footpath from Roundthwaite to Tebay and is still there.

Euston-Carlisle Express passing Tebay, Class 8 4-6-2 No. 46249 'City of Sheffield'. Pre 1952 showing old Tebay No 2 signal box on the left.   *John Marsh Photo Archive*

engine was 5552 Silver Jubilee, it was gleaming as it had just come out from a major overhaul.

One or two of my form mates were keen train spotters and they had seen it also, one lad who became my mate was Brian Holmes, his father was a driver at Oxenholme. My form teacher was Mr Wilkins, other teachers I remember were Mr Parkin (Art), Mr Grant (PT – Games), Mr Thomas (Latin), Mr Mounsey (English), Mr Dalrimple (Music) and Mr Taylor (Headmaster).

During the summer holidays it was more train spotting, fishing and rabbiting. I remember the day that electricity came to Roundthwaite and Andy Rae who had the electricity shop in Tebay wired our house up. The old Aladdin paraffin lamp was put away and only used if there was a power cut. I still have it to this day, fifty odd years later!

One very hot day in August, I thought I would go up Roundthwaite Beck grappling trout. I only had a pair of shorts on. I felt under the rocks and banks, when I felt a trout I slid my hand along its back then caught it by the gills. Once you got hold there, they could not wriggle free, that day I caught sixteen lovely trout all about eight inches, as that was the normal size for that beck. I threaded a stick through their gills as it made it easy to carry them.

During holidays I often went with dad to the signal box where ever he was at. This day he was working at Tebay No 1 Box. Tebay had three signal boxes, this one being the largest, just the job for getting train numbers. I happened to be looking out of the large window at the back when I saw about fifteen ducks dropping into the river, as the river was only about twenty-five yards from the box. I told dad and he said, 'I'll bring the gun tomorrow, they will come in there every night.' Next day I went with him again, hoping that he would get one and about the same time of day they landed again. Dad rang the Box up on either side and said, 'He was just going to the toilet if all was quiet.' It was only a few minutes when I heard 'bang-bang,' and saw some ducks fly away but sure enough dad came back with a brace of ducks. Sometimes I used to have a walk to the churchyard, which was on the same route I went when going to school, and put some flowers on mam's grave.

It had been a very wet night and the river was in flood, as I walked across the iron foot bridge I saw this man swaying from side to side, about one yard to the left then two yards to the right. Then a big splash as he fell in the river and was being swept downstream. As luck would have it, a man came rushing past me on the bridge and jumped in and saved his life. The rescuer was Edgar Corless, a signalman, who finished his rail-

way days at Burneside Crossing. The man he saved was a good customer at the Cross Keys Hotel and was carrying top weight (drunk).

They say a cat has nine lives, well I must have a bit of cat in me. Dad had a mate who farmed at Old Hutton, who he met on a trip to the T. T. Races in the Isle of Man. He visited him about once a month and I always went with him. He had a BSA 350cc at the time, this night it was freezing hard after being a showery day and on a sharp bend south of Grayrigg we parted company. Dad went one way, the bike another and me another, luckily we were none the worse, only the footrest was bent up and a small dint on the tank.

One thing I was good at, at school, was standing up in front of the class and talking about a certain subject or subjects. Mine of course was fishing and railways. I found out that the master was a keen fisherman. Most of my classmates were from the Kendal area. Raymond, my brother was also there but two classes below me. Classmates I can remember were Kenneth and Gordon Fitzgerald (the latter has a hairdressing shop in Kendal today) Barry Taylor, Brian Dobson, John Richardson, Johnathon Gibson, Keith Donoghue, Brian Jackson, Brian Morris, Peter Hine, Bill Hunt and Derek Mason. Raymond liked school more than I did and stayed until he was sixteen years old.

When the summer holidays were about to start in 1952 I was only fourteen years old, as my birthday fell just into the holidays, but I was determined that they would never see me going through those gates again.

I told my teacher this and he must have seen Mr Taylor about it, as he called me into his office. He gave me a right going over and told me the earliest I could leave was sixteen, but one of the happiest days of my life had come and I left at fourteen, ten days before my fifteenth birthday.

Facing page: Kendal Grammar School 1948.
Back row. L to R. Keith Donoghue: _____ Smith; ? ; _____ Nicholson; ? ; Keith Hine; _____ Fitzgerald and Keith Stevart.
Middle row. L to R. ? ; Derek Mason; ? ; Brian Holmes; Brian Jackson; Billy Hunt; _____ Holmes and Len Clark
Front row. L to R. ? ; ? ; Malcolm Coleman; ? ; _____ Fitzgerald (one of the twins); Form Teacher; Brian Morris; _____ Stavert?; ? : ? .

2

My First Job

I didn't know what I was going to do, but didn't care, all I knew there was no more travelling to Kendal and no more homework to do. Arther Sowerby from Ormside, near Appleby, came to farm just across from Beckside, with his wife, Rhoda and two young children, Keith and Rita. I got very friendly with them and started to help them on the farm during holidays and weekends. When I left school Arthur said I could work for him until I was old enough to get onto the railway. This pleased me no end, so on my fifteenth birthday I was working, but what I really wanted to do was get onto those steam engines. The age limit was sixteen so I had to bide my time and be patient.

I learnt to play whist when I was twelve, going once a week to Tebay. They held Whist Drives in the Ambulance Room on the Station Platform. The Ambulance Room was where a stretcher was kept in case of an accident and Tebay had a railway Ambulance Team who also practised there. They had a good team and won many competitions. The first time or two playing whist was very nerve racking. I once got a good telling off for trumping my partner's trick. People that come to mind who played whist were Harry Middleton, Mrs Thwaites, Mrs Greenhow, Billy Seed, Harry Rossel, Mrs Capstick and Mrs Sergeant (my Auntie Madge). Once I got the hang of things I started going to all the Xmas Whist Drives round about but today they seem to have been over taken by Domino Drives. I once went to Orton Xmas Whist with dad. All the ducks, chickens and geese were on the stage in sacks, squawking away! Dad won a duck and I won a box of chocolates, my first win, I went home proud as punch! When dad plucked the duck next day he said, 'There was more bloody meat on a wild 'un!' It must have been a poor one.

Arthur was the first man in Roundthwaite to make hay into pikes (small stacks). You could leave it out in the field for up to a month. To

Facing page: WD No. 90142 mixed goods heading south (up line) from Tebay with down loop going off to the left. WD – War Department.

N Stead Collection/John Marsh Photo Archive

move them he had a low flat cart that tipped up and had a wire winch on it. You put the wire rope round the pike then wound a handle and pulled it onto the cart. They were bad to fork off as they set solid and the hay was all twisted.

The year 1952 saw the last booked passenger train leave Tebay for the North East, although there were still some special passenger trains running, like the Durham Miners train that every fortnight took miners who had been ill to the convalescent home at Conishead Priory, near Ulverston, where they stayed for two weeks. In summer, trains from South Shields, Darlington took trippers to Blackpool and Southport. They all changed engines and crew at Tebay, as the North East men never worked on the W.C.M.L

Arthur had two horses and a Fordson tractor on his farm. One day he sent me off to Orton with the older horse to get it shod. This meant crossing the River Lune just below the iron bridge and then on through Old Tebay, a distance of three and a half miles to Billy Butler the blacksmith's.

We had a field house (a barn in a field) next to the main road where I used to catch the bus for school when I went to Kendal. We kept a few stirks (young cows) in one half and the other half had hay in. One morning I went in to get an armful of hay when I got hold of a man's leg instead. It was a tramp, he had stayed the night there. I came out twice as quickly as I went in. We often had a tramp called at Beckside. They were very scruffy looking, with long shaggy hair and often with a beard. Sometimes the toes of their shoes were worn right through, jackets and pants torn and they would carry a small sack on their back and a can for carrying their tea in, which they always cadged! Grandma was always very kind and gave them some tea, bread and cheese.

Jim Thompson, who just lived across the beck, kept Fell Ponies; this day he asked Arthur if he could help him to geld one (castrate). This we did in the field house. I suppose it was the practice in them days but this is what happened. First we put a sack over its head, then tied a rope round front and back legs and got it onto the ground. Arthur put a big clamp round its balls (testicles) and then burned them off with a hot iron. Then he put some salve on, jelly like ointment. Old Jim said, 'Better it than me!' Then gave a big laugh. They did lambs the same way but not quite such a performance. One job I liked was leading muck out into the field and putting it into heaps, then a day or two later scaling (spreading) it out. Arthur often used to go to Penrith Auction on a Tuesday and always took me with him.

Arthur, Rhoda, Rita
and Keith Sowerby

View from Tebay Fell, showing Grayrigg Hawes prior to motorway. Middle right of the picture is the field house where I used to stand to catch the bus to Kendal Grammar School and where I found the tramp sleeping – Roundthwaite was of to the right. Lunes Bridge Farm on the right.

This day he bought two Shorthorn heifers (a cow that had just had its first calf), a roan one and a red one. When the wagon arrived home with them they were ready to milk. The red one was a sod (bad one) it stamped and kicked so, Arthur told me to hold its tail right up in the air, this quietened her down a bit. The pair cost £28 each. It was that year that two cows from Roundthwaite made £100 each at Kendal Auction. This had never been known before in Roundthwaite, one was Arthur's, the other from Billy Parsley's herd.

Arthur, Rhoda and family later moved to Lancaster to live. The next farmer who came to farm there was called Bert Morland and is still there today and is well known for breeding Fell Ponies.

Only two months after working for Arther my dad came home from work and said I have some news for you. They want a junior porter at Low Gill Station, about five miles south of Tebay.

I was over the moon as I thought this was a start on the railway. I could always transfer to the Locomotive Department when old enough. I put an application form in to the Traffic Department and then just waited to see if I had got the job. Even though I had left school I still had my jobs to do at home with the hens. In summer we always had two or three clockers (broody hens), it was my job to look after them after we set them on eggs. We gave them ten or a dozen to sit on and I let them off to feed for about a quarter of an hour every day, then fastened them up again.

We made the boxes for the broody hens to sit in from orange boxes; today oranges come in cardboard boxes. They were just the right size, one box for two hens. We put a sod upside down in them and some straw on top. Grandma said the sod kept the moisture in. Then a board across the front of each propped up with a brick. We only let one hen off at once.

I was well into fishing by now and was a member of the Fishing Club. Dad had taught me everything I needed to know. Another job on the farm I had was to chop the turnips up in the turnip chopper; we gave some to the cows while milking them. They were very good mixed with some crushed oats or cow cake. I also chopped straw up by the same method, fed the straw into the straw chopper and wound the handle, it came out about two inches long, very good for the cows to lie on and made good muck.

Fowler 2-6-4 No. 42396 at Low Gill, a local passenger train on the down line from Ingleton to Tebay on 26 September 1953 – the year I started!
B G Tweed/N Stead Collection – John Marsh Photo Archive

During the late forties Tebay formed a concert party called, 'The Tebay Follies.' They went round all the villages, giving their first and last performance in the Institute at Tebay, this big hall was also used for whist drives, dances and pictures etc. People who took part in the concert who come to mind were May Nelson, Rose Nicholson, Harry Rooke, Roland Thomas, Edna Robertson, Betty Thornley, Jack Swindlehurst, Mr & Mrs Jimmy O'Neil, Vina Woof and Nancy McCaffee. The Institute has now been made into two houses.

Tebay was at its busiest with the railway in the early fifties. A busy junction for the North East of England, you could get a train from Tebay to Darlington, joining up with the East Coast Main Line (then the N.E.R. branch line). From Darlington you could catch a train to Scotland or London. It was known as the Railway Village, employing around two hundred people, mainly locomotive men backed up with guards, shunters, porters and signalmen. Railway houses in South Terrace and Whinfell were built by the London and North Western and the houses in North Terrace and Church Street by the North Eastern Railway. It was also known as 'Spike Island,' where that name came from nobody knows. Three houses in South Terrace were reserved for crews who had overnight to stay in Tebay, working back home the next day to Wigan and other places. Tebay had two main line signal boxes, No. 1 and No. 2, these were accompanied by Tebay No. 3, which was a small box at the north end of the N.E.R. marshalling yard. About three weeks after I applied for the job, dad came home from work to say, 'I had got it.' He also had to measure me up for a uniform. It consisted of a jacket, trousers, waistcoat, Macintosh, thick coat and a porter's cap.

I started at Low Gill in September 1952 and worked shifts, 7am till 3pm and 12 till 8pm. I used to get the train in one direction and had to pushbike the other. I biked on the 'cess.' The cess is the cinder path that is about a yard (metre) wide on the side of the track. If the wind was behind me it didn't take long, every time a train came past I stopped and put my jacket over my head in case some bits of coal fell off. Low Gill was a busy little junction, you changed there for Sedbergh and Kirkby Lonsdale. Tom Lewis was the stationmaster and he was from down country but was a grand fella. He looked after me as if I was his son. Jim Woof was the senior porter and liked his overtime and put more hours in than the mill cat. My job was to fill, trim and clean the oil lamps, clean the waiting rooms and toilets. The doors had brass knobs and I cleaned them with Brasso.

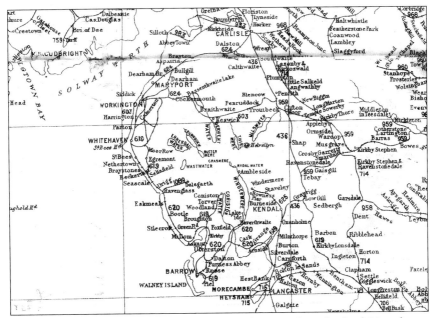

Excerpt of Bradshaw Railway Map of England, Wales & Southern Scotland. Note the many stations then!

John Cottam

Ernie Middleton in his specially adapted wagon on the Crook o' Lune Bridge.

Elsie Middleton

I had only been there about three weeks when two American ladies got off the train from Preston loaded down with luggage, they were going to Kirkby Lonsdale. They asked me if I could carry their cases across onto the branch platform, so I went for a trolley to move them. One of the ladies gave me half a crown (12½ p) in a tip. I told Jim and he said, 'You lucky bugger, I haven't had owt yet!'

The local goods pickup train, nicknamed 'Niblem' came down every day from Tebay to Ingleton and back. The crew were from Tebay so I knew them and quite often had a ride on the footplate while they did the shunting. There were quite a few sidings at Low Gill, as these places were needed for putting wagons in which had defects and weren't allowed to travel any further, quite often with hot axles. Sometimes they had to be emptied and whatever was in them put in another wagon.

The railway had a sideline that went along the roadside; this was where the local miller got his provision from, also coal etc. His name was Ernie Middleton and he lived at Davy Bank Mill, near Beckfoot. Near where he lived was the very narrow Crook 'o Lune bridge which crosses the River Lune and Ernie had to have his wagon specially adapted so that he could use it, as he often went to the farms in Howgill delivering stuff. Ernie adapted it by getting the middle two inches cut out of his front mud-guards and the sides welded back on. He also had to have the double back wheels changed to single.

There was a farmer called Neddy Grisedale who lived near the railway about half-a-mile north of Low Gill. He had a son called John and they brought two kits of milk along the cess every day to go on the train. They had a little milk bogey, John pulled with a rope at the front and Neddy pushed at the back.

When I came home on the evening train it was always the Ingleton crew, they did nothing else but go up and down the branch line with a small engine and two carriages on, a real steady number. The driver was called Jack Bird and the fireman was Dick Stobbart. They sometimes let me put some coal on. I hoped to be doing this full time in twelve months. The guard was an old chap from the south of England called Horrace Hippy.

Sedbergh has a large public school and special trains would be laid on to take the pupils and their luggage. A Tebay crew always worked this. In

Facing page: A Midland Compound 4-4-0 No 41102 which has just crossed Beckfoot viaduct and approaching Low Gill on the branch line from Sedbergh and Ingleton.
N. Stead Collection – John Marsh Photo Archive

summer there was plenty of weeding to do in the gardens around the platforms. We also had a fishpond.

The local farmer who lived just above the station at 'Scufton House', came down for his evening paper every night and always stayed half-an-hour for the crack (talk). One of the signalmen at Low Gill Box was called John Procter, commonly known as 'Bate.' Dad was very friendly with him as he enjoyed fishing. He was also friendly with a signalman from Lambrigg called Gilbert Holmes, a wonderful fly fisherman. Dad would go and visit them on his motorbike now and then.

Twelve months soon went past and I was sixteen. They wanted twelve cleaners at Tebay Loco Shed, my dream had come true and I transferred onto the Loco side. After exactly twelve months I left Low Gill.

Fowler 2-6-4T No 42314 on the down line passing Lambrigg Crossing with Gilbert Holmes standing on the steps of the signal box. Later the window of the signal box at the crossing had a wire mesh cover to protect it from coal coming of the passing tenders. Note the incident of the .22 – the door on the right is where the bullet penetrated.

3

My Next Move

This was to be an engine cleaner at Tebay Locomotive Power Shed in September 1953. To be a fireman or driver you had to serve your time, as they were very skilled jobs. Everyone started as a cleaner. Once again you were fitted out with clothes, but much different from that at Low Gill. You got two pairs of overalls and jackets made out of the same material, a hat with waterproof top, a jacket made out of thicker stuff and a mackintosh.

There were two shifts: 8am–4pm and 10pm–6am, with about six cleaners on each shift. I started on the day shift and all sorts of things were going on around you. The fitters, Alf Ellison and his mate Lance Woof, were busy doing repairs. The boiler washer was Jack Bonson who lived at Orton and he washed the engine boilers out. This had to be done every fortnight as the boilers got clogged up inside with scale. The engine was inside the shed, with no fire in and what we called as a 'dead engine'. While the engines were dead they sometimes had new fire bars put in, or brick arches rebuilt. A brick arch went from one side of the firebox to the other in a half moon shape. The firebricks all interlocked into each other and they used fire cement between them. The arch kept the fire away from the tube ends. This was a job for a cleaner to help with sometimes, all the time you were learning about a steam engine.

I used to think it was great standing up inside a firebox of a big Black Five or a Lizzie. Mind you there was always somebody waiting to play a trick on you. They would sneak up onto the footplate and close the fire hole door fastening you in. You would never know who did it. Nearly every job with new starters, a trick had to be played on them. Of course one day this happened to me. When the shift was finished and it was time to go home, we went into the cabin to collect our bait boxes, nearly all bait boxes were the tin type with a handle on top in those days. I grabbed mine and the table came as well, some smart bugger had nailed it to the table, of course nobody would split who did it.

Tebay Station staff in 1950.
L to R: Howard Nicholson, an engineer from Lancaster(name unknown),
Harry Swainbank, Ronnie Morgan, Arthur Grayland, Roach Nicholson, Ken Thornton,
Martha Wilson, Mr Cresswell – Station Master, Chris Wills, Wilf O'Neill,
Norman Sowerbutts, Edwin Nelson, James O'Neill, James Brunskill, Joe Harrison
and Harold Ritson.

Just about the same time as the trick was played on me, a young lad
started on the platform as a porter. There was a shunting pole stood
against the wall. A shunting pole has a long straight pole with a crook on
the end used by shunters to couple and uncouple wagons. Anyway the
station foreman played a trick on him, as he was a new starter. He sent
him to wind up the station clock. This was the crack for a week or two
among the staff.

The material used to clean an engine was a bundle of cloths, a bucket
with oil and paraffin mixed in and a scraper. First job was to scrape all the
muck off the wheels and motions. You would split into three groups.
Two do the wheels, two the boiler and two the tender. Sometimes the
engine was in steam with a very low fire on, other times it was dead. One
lad put the stuff on and the other polished it off. The shed boss was properly called the shed master. He did all the office work, selecting which
engine went on which run and the rostering of men. He came round to

Tebay Shed 1958

Tebay Depot – the first shed was built in 1855 at Loups Fell and held one loco to bank Lancaster and Carlisle trains up Shap. Later shed opened in 1861 costing £2,600. Railway cottages were not built until later and crews slept the first winter in temporary wooden sheds inside the engine shed. Locos were coaled for many years by hand before a mechanical coaling plant was built.

When I started in 1953 the shed was known as 11E and sadly closed on 1 January 1968.

In this picture there are two banking engines on the right – both Fowlers No 42396 and 42424. On the left is a WD. The ash pit can be seen between the rails on the foreground and various tools – paddle, pricker and tongs used by the fireman. *N. Stead*

45

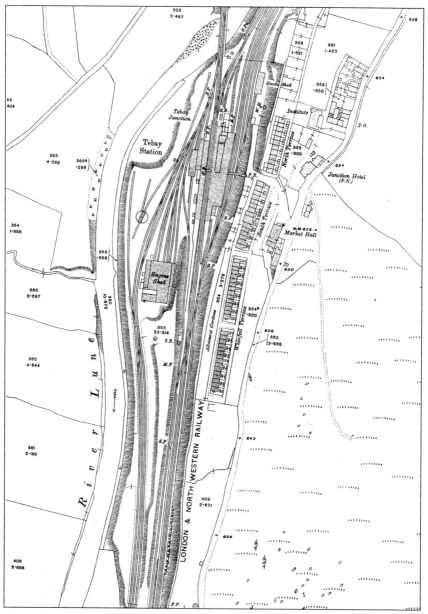

Excerpt of Tebay Station from 1915 Ordnance Survey Map.

Kendal Local Studies/John Marsh Photo Archive

see if you were cleaning the engine properly. His name was Mr Warren and he lived at Low Gill. At the end of my first week he had me, along with some other lads, into his office. He said that by March when the holiday roster went up they would be very short of firemen, so he wanted us to take it in turns, having a ride from Tebay to Shap summit on the footplate of the banking engine, also when we were on night turn. This was good news for us all; everything seemed to be running right for me.

One day Alan Wharton and Jack Balmer had booked on for the 1.45pm bank. The job of these banking engines was to assist any goods train that carried more than nineteen wagons up to the top of Shap summit 916 feet above sea level, which were not fully fitted throughout with brakes worked from the loco. Some goods trains only had a third fitted, some had none. The bank engines were also there for protection in case a train's coupling broke. This they did by closely going behind the train once it had come to a stand, then pushed them up, they did not attach onto the train, as when they reached the top the driver just shut the power off and came to a halt while the train carried on to Carlisle. The Tebay loco crossed over on to the up line and came back to base. The line going north was always called the down line and the one going south was the up line.

Anyway about 2.30pm this goods train whistled for assistance, as it went past the shed. It looked to be in poor form, as it was belching black smoke out and not a sign of steam coming from the safety valves. The safety valve is where the steam blows out of when it reaches a certain pressure. This is known as 'blowing off.' Alan asked me if I wanted to ride up with them, of course I jumped at it. This was the very first time out on the main line for me. I just stood in a corner of the cab and took it all in, watching every move that the fireman made. Jack Balmer was noted for hammering an engine; some drivers were very light on them. We came back down the bank at a tremendous speed, I think Jack was trying to frighten me, I reckon when we went past Scout Green signal box we were doing 80mph. What a tale I had to tell when I got home! Other lads that came to mind were Jimmy Bell, Alan Nicholson, Tony Whitehead, Terence Whitehead, Derek O'Neil and Denis Potter.

The next week we were on night shift 10pm–6am. It was the same thing as on days, six of us to clean an engine. It was fairly quiet on nights inside the shed. All the loco's were back in after their daily run, only the hissing of the three loco's on banking duties could be heard. Once we got started we never stopped till our loco was clean, as there was no shed master to bother us. We usually could get two to three hours kip. Also this was a perfect chance to get more knowledge about firing. I took every chance and by now I was going up Shap quite often. It was totally different at night, the glare of the fire was blinding. Sparks came out of the chimney into the night sky.

Tebay only had about a dozen loco's allocated. Every loco had a number – hence the phrase getting engine numbers. Every engine had a class and some had names eg. Royal Scot, Jubilee, Coronation 5 Mixed Traffic, Fowler's, Fairburn's and so on. All these were different classes. Tebay had four or five 2-6-4 Class 4 Fowlers. Two-six-four means two front bogie wheels, six driving wheels and four trailing wheels. Four 0-6-0 Class 4 F's and two 2-6-2 Class 3 and also others on loan for various lengths of time, sometimes Black Fives or Super Ds for general purposes. The Fowlers were used to haul as many as four or five coke trains a day from the North East to Lindal, near Barrow. During a journey a fireman might shovel five or six tons of coal into the firebox of his loco. At the time we had 4469, 4292, 3896 and 4083. The 4083 was noted as being a bad steamer and the footplate staff had their own 'Jimmies' to assist that loco to steam. This was a specially shaped piece of steel that they fitted across the top of the blast pipe to spread the blast and create more vacuums. This was removed at the end of the shift.

If we were on night shift cleaning during September to November we would pop across to the river only a hundred yards away and get one for the pot, unless someone asked for a salmon. We could be back in the shed in ten minutes. Other duties for cleaners on day turn were to help George Capstick on ash pits. These were long pits between the rails where the loco fire was dropped into, every time the loco was made dead, usually after a day's run. Also the ash pan under the loco had to be cleaned out daily, as did the smoke box, which was at the front end under the chimney. These were very hot and dirty jobs especially if a strong wind was blowing. The smoke box ash was very hot and small.

Usually there was a driver and fireman on each shift who did nothing else after an engine returned from its daily run but to get it loaded up with coal and water, turn it on the turntable if necessary, drop the fire and clean out the ash pan and smoke box. These men were called Tommy Roberts, Bill Hayes and Fred Simpson, all drivers; they had various mates, sometimes I did that job later on. To lift fire bars out you had some large tongs and to lift the fire out a shovel with a long handle, this was called a paddle. Other tools were a bent dart and a pricker.

It was soon March and by this time I had put my hand to the shovel many times, together with other duties, so was ready for the big day, to be

Fowler 2-6-4T (banking engine) prepares to buffer up behind the freight train and assist its passage up Shap summit.

Early BR No 45191 Stanier 5 M.T. 4-6-0 on the down line near Tebay on Dillicar Troughs. The water was piped to the troughs from a large water tank at Tebay Station.

John Marsh Photo Archive

passed out fit to fire. When a cleaner was passed out for firing duties he became known as a 'cleaner fireman' and had to have many turns in, before coming a fully booked fireman. This took a long time.

By this time I was sort of grown up and started socialising a lot more in the village and I also started to follow the Lunesdale Foxhounds, which I still do to this day. Walter Parkin was the huntsman and a gentleman he was too. I went as often as I could when they were hunting locally. I started going to dances, as they had them quite often in the Village Institute and other villages. The main dances were the Hunt Balls. A Hunt Ball was held in every village once a year, where girls entered to take part in the 'Miss Lunesdale Competition'. One girl represented each village, then at the end of the season a final was held at Morecambe. This was in the Winter Gardens, dozens of buses took people from all parts. What a night this was for country people, it was on this night that all the girls who had won at village Hunt Balls were judged again and the winner was crowned as 'Miss Lunesdale,' who got a sash and a good prize.

You can talk about paying for your learning well I did one night. Jackie Neil and Albert Young, who were firemen that I knew very well, asked me if I was going to the dance on Saturday night. I said, 'That I could do.' So arranged to meet them in 'The Cross Keys Inn' at 8pm, of course still under drinking age but nobody bothered then. Anyway I went in and sure enough Albert and Jackie were stood at the bar, Albert drinking a bottle of stout and Jackie drinking a pint of bitter. I only had ten shillings on me, which I suppose was a bit in them days, so I asked them what they wanted to drink. Jackie said he would have a Mousec, Albert in his up style voice said, 'Yes, I will have one too.' I did not have a clue what it was but they said I had to try one, which I did. The landlord then was Sid Woof. He said, "Seven shillings and sixpence please." I only had two shillings and sixpence left for the night. I soon found out that Mousec came in a small bottle, similar to a barley wine and was very strong and expensive!

Mr and Mrs Wilkinson were the licensees at the Cross Keys prior to Sid Woof, and they had two sons, John and David. They went to Preston to live around 1953. David married a girl called Jill and came back to Tebay to live with their two daughters and a son, Mark, Janet and Karen. David and Jill still live at Tebay on Galloper Park and Janet later became my daughter-in-law.

During the forties and early fifties Tebay had a Brass Band consisting mainly of railwaymen. Names that come to mind were, Jack Horsley (band master), Jack Blair, Harold Rae, George Todd, my uncle Nat

Sargeant and George Goldsmith. Whist drives were held often which I never missed going to. I was having a very busy social life by now. Tebay Fishing Club of which I was a member from about the age of ten, held an annual meeting and social event every year in the Junction Hotel. This year I was on night shift so I knew there was no rush, I got one of my mates to book me on. I went to work about midnight quite full of beer. Try doing that today, it would mean instant dismissal.

Tebay had a man called John Thornborrow who worked in insurance but was also an artist. Jack as he was known as, always had paintings on show in the bay window of his sitting room, except that is on Sundays. Jack was a strong Methodist but a real gentleman. His son Bernard lives only a few houses below where his dad lived in Mount Pleasant.

Alan Wharton came to live at Whinfell Terrace, Tebay along with mother, Nora, and father, Jack, younger brother Colin and sisters Doris, Jean and Margery. I got very friendly with them and Colin has been my best mate from a very early age, what a good pal. I went to Tebay School with Margery. Jack worked as a ganger on the Permanent Way.

This day in March 1954 I met Mr Warren the shed master and he told me he was going to pass me out for firing. It was with one of the early shift crew, Charlie Taylor, the driver and Stan Stainton was the fireman. Mr Warren told them what was going to happen, so Stan just stood in the corner of the footplate as if he weren't there. The engine was number 2424 and I was lucky as it had not been long back from a major overhaul. It was easy to make steam on and did not use as much water as some. A heavy goods train pulled out of the siding dragging about thirty-nine wagons all loaded; off we went behind him and up the bank. Mr Warren was stood in the other corner behind the driver, everything went well and I was full of confidence. When we arrived back the boss said, "Well done," I had passed for firing on the bank engines only of course. To be passed for main line trains, an inspector from Carlisle came. I went home that day like a dog with two tails.

Usually the morning shift was the busiest with three bankers doing something like five or six trips each. The first shift was at 4.15 am then 5.15 am and 5.45 am. The first freight train of the day was usually from Ribble sidings, Preston that arrived at 4.30 am and then we had a steady

Facing page: Relaying by hand at Tebay in 1954. No shortage of labour. Everything was done by hand. It took twenty men to lift a 60' rail. No high visibility clothing. Penrith had two relaying groups with thirty men in each. Lancaster had at least one such group. They spent their time doing nothing else but relaying they did not do maintenance.

LMS Train for Kirkby Stephen c. 1952. An Ivatt 2-6-0 'Mogul' 1946, No 46475.
N Stead Collection/John Marsh Photo Arhive

Cross Keys, Tebay in May 1993. Where I had my first drink!

flow of traffic from other yards like Bosford Hall (Crewe), Willesden, Camden, Edge Hill, Bamfurlong and many others.

The following week I was marked up as firing all week on the 1.45pm shift. My driver was Joe Glover, an ex Wigan man, who came to live at Tebay. He was a grand mate and good to work with. In the fifties, the goods traffic on the railways was enormous, everything went by rail. A milk train ran every day from Carlisle to London, also fish and meat trains from Scotland to the capital. Mondays and Tuesday were very busy for banana trains running from Garston Docks in Liverpool to Scotland, probably four or five each day and these were hanging in the vans and were green. They had to have heat on all the time; this was piped from the engine, as it was on passenger trains. One night, I was on the 9.15pm bank when a banana train had taken a van off at Tebay that morning with a hot axle. One of the day shift bankers stood hooked onto it all day providing heat. We did the same for the full eight hours at night, never moved a wheel, the driver George Marsden, who was another Lancashire man, slept most of the time and all I had to do was keep a low fire on and make sure the steam heater gauge was up to the mark. Sometimes it was a very hard job, other times easy, like that one.

Driving and firing an engine was similar in a way to driving a car, and of course it all depended on what condition the coal was in. Yorkshire coal was the best. The age had come for me to be old enough to drive. So I bought this old Ford Eight car from a farmer called Jimmy Hewitt, from Crosby Ravensworth. I met him at a dance at Orton and told him I wanted a car. He said it was in the barn and had not been started for a while. I went over the next day to look at it, it was covered in hay dust and you could tell it had been there for some time, but the body looked well. I brought it back to Roundthwaite, the tax had run out and I had no insurance. I should have been locked up, but I soon got that fixed, it was my first car my pride and joy. I used to go all over to dances in it, with 'L' plates on, with one of my mates who could drive.

All I had to do now was pass my test. I soon learned, I was used to driving tractors and it wasn't long before I went for my test. We had to go to Kendal and report to somewhere on Sandes Avenue. There was a lot of snow and ice on the road but I was full of confidence, maybe too full. The man took me round the top of Sandylands Estate. I think he would want a clean pair of underpants when he got back. I think I put the fear of God up him. I could tell by his actions that I had failed. When we arrived back at Sandes Avenue he ticked his sheet and failed me on two things. Going far too fast for the road conditions and the three-point turn. I went another twice before passing.

One day at work I was talking to one of my mates, Tom Greenhow, who went with me to a lot of dances. I told him I had had a good do with the salmon the two days previous. I had caught eight with the rod and was going to take them to two hotels in Morecambe, which had bought them of me before. He said he would have a ride with me. Off we went, the car seemed to be running okay until we went up Docker Brow south of Grayrigg. We got about a third of the way up and it spluttered to a halt. We freewheeled to the bottom and tried again twice, it wouldn't have it. So I said, 'We will try it in reverse.' It went up no trouble and continued to Morecambe and we got back in time for a pint at the Junction to spend our fish money.

Tebay always had a useful football team, as they still do to this day. Players that come to mind from those days are Rupert Wills, Edwin Akrigg, Brian Lord, Tommy Rudd, Maurice Medcalf, Gordon and Raymond Robertson, Billy Pattinson, Jackie Neil, Wilf Draper and Keith Hawkins. It was always a grudge match against local rivals, Shap. You could bet one or two would be sent off for fighting. Some of the Shap spectators were very biased, I remember one woman hitting a Tebay supporter over the head with her brolly. Nearly every time there was a dance at Orton or Shap lads landed over and there was sure to be a scrap. Police Sergeant Ivison was the Shap sergeant and he was always stood outside, never booked anyone just gave them a clout and told them to be on their way with a grin on his face. He was a proper copper!

The Cross Keys Inn was most popular on Sunday nights. For the first hour Sid Woof did nothing but pull pints of beer, as around twenty of us went in to play darts. Those who played darts at the time were Harry Preston, myself, Harry Davies, George and Alan Carruthers, Jackie Neil, Hubert Gilpin, Ernie High, Billy Pattinson, Jim Nicholson, Eric Murphy and many more. Then for the last hour we went up into the top room where Billy Woof would be playing the piano, we would have a good old singsong. A man from Kendal came up quite often called Harold Kirk. He married a girl from Tebay called Vera O'Neil. Harold was a tremendous whistler, his favourite song was, 'If I was a blackbird, I'd whistle and sing.' On the dartboard we would play, Sergeants, Slip-up, 301 up or Shang Hi. I was getting involved in all sorts, I started playing darts for the Junction in the League, then the Keys, then the George at Orton, Brian Lord was the landlord up there, he was a Tebay lad, his dad Jack was signalman in Tebay No 2 Box.

Fireman Martin Proctor and driver Jack Bond in the Locomotive Shed Office, Tebay in
1950s   *Martin Proctor*

Group of employees at Loco Dept in 1954.
L to R: Terence Whitehead, Joe Winder, David Scott, Frank Haygarth, Tony
Whitehead, Tom Greenhow, Jack Greenhow, Brian? Tinkler, Tommy Rudd, Charlie
Udall, Jim Douthwaite, Bob Currugh, ? ;Martin Proctor, Tommy Whittam and Jim
Lewis.   *Martin Proctor*

A busy scene at Tebay Station on 4 August 1954. No 46121 down Manchester-Glasgow Express. Royal Scot 4-6-0 'Highland Light Infantry City of Glasgow Regiment.' Wagons full of coal in the shed and another loco waiting with goods to enter.

John Marsh Photo Archive

Tebay Football Team 1965-66 Season
L to R – back row: Gordon Robertson, ? , Cyril Hodgson, Brian Lord, Keith Hawkins, Maurice Medcalfe and Geoff Bellas.
Front row: Alan Mawson, Raymond Robertson, Tony Bellas (ball boy), Billy Pattinson, Ted Jackson (Linesman Maurice Coates).

Tebay Station was a very busy place in the forties and fifties, about four passenger trains stopping each way. The 12.30pm passenger train that stopped always had a large Palethorpes Sausage Van on next to the engine, and very often a long parcel carriage loaded with young calves. There was a man called Joe Askew who lived in Old Tebay. He had a very lame leg and always had a stick. He collected fish off the southbound early morning train and loaded a couple of fish boxes onto his handcart. He layed his stick across the shafts and somehow used to lean on the cart as he pushed it, taking fish around the village. People from Carlisle often used to send racing pigeons on the train to Tebay, then they were let off to fly back. We quite often went on the train to watch Preston North End play football when Tom Finney used to play, or sometimes went to watch Blackpool or Carlisle United.

The village shops were also busy, two Co-ops, Doug Majors a cobblers, Mrs Bloomers sweet shop, a garage, a bank, Post Office, two green grocers, shoe shop, chip shop and café. It was always a joke in Tebay, 'Why was Tebay like a woman?' Answer, 'It had Bloomers half way up!' Today we have nothing except for a small shop in Old Tebay Filling Station and café, which is used mainly by wagon drivers as it is a change-over place for them. It also gets many buses calling in on their way to and from Blackpool and Morecambe, mainly in summer. At the time of writing this book we have lost our Post Office, the nearest one now being at Orton three miles away.

The time came round for me to be 'passed out to fire' on the Main Line. If you passed, that meant you could go anywhere and Tebay had some good runs, to Carlisle, Preston, Barrow, Hellifield and Blackpool. A footplate inspector arrived from Carlisle by the name of John Craig. I had seen him before but not to talk to. He was a big man about 6' 3" tall and wore a long black coat and black bowler hat. The train we were going to work to Carlisle was in the down loop. A loop is a sideline next to the main line and slow trains are put in a loop to let others pass. My driver was Wilf Rae. The train had come from Crewe with Crewe men at the controls. As I climbed up the steps and onto the footplate the fireman said, "She's a good 'un." I said, "I bloody well hope so, look who's coming behind me, John Craig."

The engine fire did not look so bad, as sometimes if an engine has come a long way and the coal was bad, the fire could be clinkered up and looked rather blue and dead. It was Class 5 M.T. number 5431. M.T. stands for mixed traffic, as these engines were made for both passenger and goods work. They were the best all rounder there was. The coal was

quite well back in the tender so I got in and shovelled some forward, while we were stood. Some loco's had steam coal pushers on so that would spare the fireman that job. Two or three expresses passed us, then the signal came off for us to go. We only had to go a quarter-of-a-mile then we stopped for a bank engine to come into the rear of us. A loud crow from the rear engine and a crow from us in return and we were off heading for Carlisle Upperby Yard. A crow is a type of whistle that drivers use. John put me at ease before we set off out of the loop, he said, "You will be okay, don't bother about me," and he was right. We made Carlisle no trouble, what an experience that was, something I had prayed for since I was a small boy. He said, "You have passed, no problem, I just have to ask you a few rules out of the rule book." These I had swotted up well before. I had passed another milestone.

During the summer of 1955 Oxenholme Shed was very short of staff so I was sent on loan for three weeks. I got quite a bit of overtime each day so was making good money. They had some nice runs, Windermere to Morecambe both ways, Preston and of course on the bank engines which pushed trains up to Grayrigg. One job was shunting all day in Kendal Yard. Just then Kendal was a very busy place on the railway and one day I was on the Kendal shunt. My mate was Togo Swanton, I don't know if Togo was his proper name as we had a driver at Tebay called Bob Wills who always got 'Togo'. I met many more friends down there. Togo never wore overalls, always grey trousers, and never seemed to get dirty. We shunted all day long backwards and forwards as stuff came in from the town and this was mainly made up of 'K' Shoes, snuff and Kendal Mint Cake. Coal and oil came in for the town. The worst part about that job was we were right besides Cumsteys where they used to render fat down. On a hot day in summer as this one was, the smell was terrible! Around 5pm a goods train from Windermere would arrive and pick up all the traffic for the south, from Kendal, then we would push him up the quite steep gradient to Oxenholme.

One of the highlights of my career on the Loco Department was another day at Oxenholme when I was on the afternoon bank. My driver was Kenneth Kirk, father to Harold who I mentioned earlier. He again was a grand mate. This day the down Royal Scot wired through from Lancaster that he was doing badly and wanted assistance through to Shap summit. That would spare him stopping at Tebay as well. So we had to

Milk and parcels northbound on Dillicar Troughs. An X-sign was illuminated at night to tell enginemen when to lower their water scoop.

N. Stead Collection/John Marsh Photo Archive

couple onto the front of the Royal Scot loco that was being hauled by Coronation Class No 6234 Duchess of Abercorn. It is very rare that this type of loco should be steaming badly. Our engine was a Class 4 number 2301 and a good one. I had it on the mark of blowing off point almost all the way. Once we passed Grayrigg it was fairly level going through the Lune Valley until we reached Tebay. About a mile below Tebay Station were some water troughs (Dillicar Troughs) where trains picked up water at speed. They were a quarter of a mile long and the troughs stood just below rail level in between the two rails. The fireman's job was to turn this handle as quickly as possible when entering the troughs; this let a scoop down into the water and the force with the speed sent the water up into the tender. There was a gauge inside the cab to show how full the tank was, so when this gauge nearly reached the top you had to turn this handle clockwise very quickly, otherwise the water would come out of the top of the tender and cover half of the nearest carriage. If the train was double headed as we were, the train engine puts his scoop down first, then half way along the troughs the front engine dropped his scoop as we did. We were going at a very fast speed through Tebay and were soon up at Shap summit, there we stopped, unhooked and drew into the siding and the Royal Scot was once again on its way to Glasgow. As it went past us the driver gave a smile and put his thumb up, to say thank you. We then crossed over to the up line and leisurely went back to Oxenholme.

The drivers at Oxenholme who come to my mind are: Dennis Boardley, Bob Holmes, Jack Holmes whose son I went to school with at Kendal, Eric Armer, Togo Swanton, Ken Kirk, Tom Thuliss and Joe Mitchell.

By this time my brother, Raymond had left school and gone into the Police Force as a cadet starting at Appleby, then six months later at Kendal. He had to go into lodgings and it was there that he met his wife Doreen Potter, who lived on Rinkfield Estate at the south end of the town.

One day at work two or three of my mates decided they would go to a dance at Kendal. They were held in the Parish Hall next to the Parish Church at the south end of town. We met in the Junction Hotel and had a few beers, we then called at the Dun Horse in Kendal for some more, eventually arriving at the dance. We went in my Ford Eight of course, four of us, Colin Wharton, Lance Greenhow, Edwin Akrigg and myself. On the way back we felt hungry, so decided to go up the A6 road and call

Local passenger train leaving Oxenholme for Windermere. I walked the line as well as fired various engines along here. *N. Stead Collection/John Marsh Photo Archive*

Jungle Café (now caravan sales) pictured in the 1950s. A popular 24-hour café on the busy A6 (main north south route) popular with wagon and bus drivers.

John Marsh Photo Archive

at the Jungle Café, a very well known café for wagon drivers, open all day and night. We were going for a good supper. The Jungle Café was just north of Selside. About ¾ mile south of the café tragedy struck us. I was going too fast round this bend and got into a hell of a wobble and threw the car onto its side. Two of my mates went through the roof and all I could remember was sparks and dust flying. The car went on its side for twenty-five yards and luckily came to a halt near a gate into a field. Amazingly nobody was any the worse. The police arrived, also many wagon drivers who helped us to right the car and get it into the field.

The policeman was very helpful and of course asked us all sorts of questions. He was from Kendal and took us just up the road to the café for a drink of coffee and something to eat. He also had a cup of coffee with us. He said he would take us back to Tebay but had not enough petrol in so we went back to Kendal with him. He dropped us off at the Police Station in Lowther Street. Who should be on duty but Sergeant Harold Watson, who we all knew, as he was a keen hunting man with the Lunesdale Pack and knew us quite well. The first words he said, 'What have you Tebay Buggers been up to?' We told him the tale. He said, 'How are you getting back to Tebay at this time of day, half past two on a Sunday morning?' Tebay was twelve miles from Kendal. He got us a lift to Shap summit on the A6 in a coach loaded with football supporters going home to Carlisle. We got a bank engine back down to Tebay, after having to wait in the Signal Box at Shap summit for about two hours. When we got onto the loco, who should be driving but Togo Wills, his face lit up when we told him what happened. We got home at around 6am, quite a costly night out for me, also my pride and joy was a write off. Dad gave me a good telling off but I think he was only too glad we were none the worse. He went with me the next afternoon, with Joe Bell from Orton in his cattle wagon, to bring it back. Joe was one of the local men who took cattle to the local markets. To see that car you just could not believe anyone got out alive, another one of my nine lives gone. That evening I met Jim Thompson who lived opposite Beckside, he had heard about the carry on. He said to me, "Now as garn to tell thee summat, them that drives fast niver drives lang!"

If a loco is dead it takes about seven hours to get full steam up. This is the job of the steam raiser and Bob Ritson was ours. This is the method he used. Put a good layer of coal all around the firebox except for a two-foot square in the middle. Then get about six fire lighters on a firing shovel, light them and place them in the bare bit of the firebox, then just place a small amount of coal on top. The fire will then gradually spread.

The blower that creates a draught underneath will not work until a certain amount of steam is raised. He worked regular nights 10pm–6am and had about seven or eight loco's to look after. He was a quiet but rather nervous man and when it was getting towards 5 November, some young lad would wait until he was on the footplate in semi-darkness and then throw a lighted banger or a jumping Jack on to frighten him.

One day we were working an empty wagon train back from Preston to Tebay. My mate the driver was Frank Ormrod, who unfortunately died just as I started writing this book. He had a Class 4 engine the same as we used on the banking duties, rather too small for the job we were doing. It was a nasty wet day and the rail was greasy, as we used to call it when wet. Approaching Carnforth, we were sent into No 1 loop, as Carnforth had two loop lines side by side. We were going pretty fast and I said to Frank, "You aren't going to stop mate?" Frank said, "I think we're OK." Just as he braked harder, the engine started to slide. Picked up its wheels in railway terms, so he had no control and the weight of the train was pushing us. As bad luck happened, there was another goods train pulling out of Loop No 2 crossing our path onto the main line. The next thing was a very loud clatter and bang as we smashed into the other train causing one hell of a derailment. I thought our loco was going to go over on its side as it rocked so badly. Luck was with us there, because if it had gone over we would have been killed or badly hurt. Altogether twelve wagons were derailed, some smashed to pieces. This caused a terrible amount of delay to other trains, as the steam crane had to come to clear the line. A loco was always called 'she'. The track was called the road. Hence the saying 'she was off the road' if becoming derailed. Yet another life gone!

Tebay had three jobs per day carrying coke from Durham to Millom Iron Works, the North East men came as far as Tebay then we took over. This was a nice run in summer time but a very hard job. Leaving Tebay heading south we left the W.C.M.L. at Hincaster Junction and went down the single line to Arnside, where it met up with the Carnforth to Barrow line, along the sea front past Grange-over-Sands, Cark and to Plumpton Junction where we stopped for a banking engine, as we were now approaching Ulverston on a steep gradient. Ulverston Station was mostly covered in except for where the track was. The beat of that engine and the roar was tremendous. This particular day my mate was Teddy Wills. We went as far as Lindal Ore Sidings, just north of Barrow-in-Furness. There we left our loaded train and crossed over to the opposite side where a train load of empties were waiting for us to take back to Tebay. Before we were homeward bound, the engine had to be turned on the turntable, the fire cleaned and the tender filled up with water. Then we were on our way, an easy run until we reached Arnside and up the single line again. The signalman at either end would give you a token as you passed the box allowing you to enter the single line. The token was like a round hoop that the signalman held out for you to catch on your arm. From Arnside it was all up hill to Grayrigg about six miles north of Oxenholme. As we passed Hincaster Box to join the W.C.M.L. again the signalman would grab to take the token from me. This was a very hard slog up to Grayrigg, usually with thirty-eight empties behind you. The loco mostly used was a 0-6-0 Class 4F. This day it was 4292. The tender was piled high with coal before we left Tebay and on arriving back at Tebay Depot only a barrow full was left. A wonderful day's work and it was a great pleasure to me doing it.

The week after this trip, a letter was waiting for me when I got home. It was to say that I had to report to Carlisle Castle for a medical to do National Service. I was expecting it sooner or later, but it was a letter I could do without. Anyway I passed A1 and soon got my papers to enrol. I knew my job would be waiting when I finished in two years' time but to leave those loco's and the River Lune was a disaster to me. So I had to go and do my bit in the spring of 1956.

Me in uniform in 1956 at Aldershot.

On my cooking course at
Penicuik in 1956.

4

Army Days

I was only a country boy really, never been away from home to stay except on my holidays with my Grandma and Granddad Clark at Shap. I knew nothing about the army; only what other mates had told me and that didn't seem so good. I went into the Army Catering Corps and had to report to Ramilles Barracks at Aldershot in Hampshire, on this particular Monday before 3pm.

On the Sunday night dad took me down to Carnforth to catch the 9.30pm Barrow to Euston train. It was a terrible feeling just like going into the unknown. On arriving at London there were many more lads doing the same thing and I soon got talking to them. We had to cross London to get to Waterloo Station for a train to Aldershot. At Waterloo the station was packed with lads going to join up as Aldershot was a very big garrison town. After arriving I was kitted out and went to our billet. I was to be there for six weeks square bashing, route marches, assault coursing and such like.

Aldershot was six weeks of hell. Everywhere you went you were marched, even to the pay office, and then had to salute for our one pound a week. I had five haircuts in six weeks, not that I wanted one, and had to pay for them. That barber must have been making a fortune as he was a civilian.

Our barrack square was about the size of a football pitch and was tarmac. On parade this day the lad next to me dropped his rifle, so the Sergeant made him run round the outside of the square holding the rifle above his head, and just kept shouting, 'faster, faster,' at him. At 6am the Sergeant on duty came round to say in no uncertain terms, 'Get out of bed!' If you weren't out in five minutes the bed was tipped over with you underneath it. I always was one of the first up, so I got the hot water for a wash and shave before it went cold. Every night you sat on the end of your bed cleaning your belt with Blanco and Brasso for the buckles. We got two pair of boots and what we did was heat a spoon handle up then press it on the toe end of the boot, this took all the pimples out and made it smooth, then came the spit and polish, rub some boot polish on then spit on it and keep rubbing it in. In time you could just about see to shave in them, they were gleaming. All your kit was folded up neatly and stacked on top of your locker in a special way. If it were not right when the officer came to inspect, the Sergeant would throw it the full length of the room. A saying he quite often used was, 'You may break your mother's heart but you won't break mine!' You had to put your bed clothes folded in a square pack every morning, a sheet, a blanket, another sheet, another blanket, then a blanket wrapped right round. If it wasn't done right, it was knocked off the bed.

After the six weeks had passed, a passing out parade took place. I used to write home and ask for all the local news, which I got. After passing out the next day we travelled by overnight train to Edinburgh, to start a three-month cookery course, at least I saw plenty of loco's on my way. I remember as the train passed Berwick-on-Tweed the railway was very close to the sea and the sun was just rising from the east and shining on the water. What a lovely night. The next ride was not as comfortable, as six army trucks were waiting to take us to the camp at a place called Penicuik, about twelve miles from Edinburgh. There were about thirty of us. It was to be our home for three months, after a short while we were allowed home for the weekend. One good thing, I only paid a quarter fare on the trains.

When I arrived home I must have sat for an hour answering questions, dad and grandma were asking. Then at night it was to the Junction Hotel to meet my old mates, a few games of darts and away to a dance some-where. It still irked me that I had left a job where I was making good money, about £12 per week and in the army, I got about a pound and out of that, paid for boot polish, Brasso, Blanco and any other things needed.

I soon learned one thing though, never volunteer for anything. One day at Aldershot the Sergeant asked, 'Put your hands up who can ride a bike?' So of course I was one of them. He said, 'Go and get me some cig-arettes!' The same thing happened at Penicuik but I made sure I didn't put my hand up.

Life was slightly better in Scotland but we still had to do guard duty, cross country runs and shooting on the rifle ranges. One good thing, the food was far better. I soon got friendly with a lad who came from down south, he was asking me about country life, he hadn't a clue. We were allowed home about once a month by now, so that wasn't too bad, so I told him next time I go home for the weekend he could go with me, this he agreed to. I thought I would show him what country life was all about.

The first day at home was Saturday and the Lunesdale Pack were hunting near to Tebay. I took him to the hunt. Our luck was in, he saw a very good hunt and also the kill. That afternoon I thought I would go out with the ferret, I knew where there was a good set or two (rabbit holes). So off we went, although I never reckoned to go ferreting in the afternoon but it was a nice day and I wanted to show him as much as I could in such a short time. We went to this set that looked as if it was being used well. Before we arrived I told him that he must keep dead quiet, if you made any noise the rabbits would not bolt. There were five holes in all and I put the nets on and then put the ferret in. He kept asking me questions and I kept motioning him to be quiet. Just then I saw a rabbit come to a net but shot back down the hole. I knew they weren't going to bolt. After a while the ferret came out with fur in its claws and went back in again. I lay on the ground with my ear on the earth, I could hear the ferret banging. I was a bit annoyed because I had warned him about noise. He asked, 'Why wont they come out?' I said, 'Because you wouldn't keep your trap shut!' I dug in where I could hear the ferret and it wasn't too deep, the ferret was there. I could see the back of a rabbit, so I caught the ferret and put him back in the box. I grabbed this rabbit and gave it one bat behind the ears then dug just a little more and pulled another five out. They were all in a dead end, no escape hole for them. You should have seen the lad's face. We tried another set and got two more. We had quite a long way to walk home, so I gave him the rabbits to carry. I carried the spade, ferret box and nets. That was his penalty for not keeping quiet, as eight rabbits can weigh quite heavy.

Next thing was teatime, we had a good tea then I thought I would go and wait for carrion crows coming into this wood I knew very well. A carrion crow is a nasty bird, which takes out lambs eyes as soon as they are born and eats ground birds eggs and their young. I always shot quite a few each year. I told him now this time it is a must that you don't talk, otherwise they would not come near. I got him rigged up with a dark balaclava and dark jacket. It was almost dark before they came into the trees to roost, as they are a very wary bird. I saw one come and settle, I don't think my friend saw it, so I shot at it and it dropped dead. I think the bang off the 12 bore shot gun gave him a fright. It was the only one we got but it would be an experience for him I expect.

Next day, Sunday we had to be at Carlisle Station to catch the 5.30pm train to Edinburgh, so our time was getting short now. I thought the only thing left now was a couple of hours fishing. It was autumn time so the fishing season was still in. We caught two nice trout on a quill minnow for bait. I always fish for trout with this sort of bait. So dad took us to Carlisle to catch the train, it was the 'The Mid Day Scot' hauled by engine number 6200 named 'The Princess Royal.' These are the sorts of things I never forget and of course I was very happy near these locos. Sometimes these classes of engines were poor steamers and quite often called at Tebay for a banking engine. This he did at Beattock, which has a steep gradient. Half way up to Beattock summit I put my head out of the window and watched the 'Iron Horse', blasting away sending plenty of black smoke out. I wonder what sort of a tale that lad told his parents next time he went home.

After three months cookery training I was a qualified cook and got the chance of being posted abroad to Tripoli but I said, 'No,' as I was thinking of Grandma Sergeant who was getting quite old and frail, who I loved so much. What was the good of me being thousands of miles away if something happened to her, I was thinking. So I was posted back down south to Farnborough in Hampshire. From there they put me into a pool gang going to different camps where they were short of cooks. I visited twelve camps in thirteen months. One of these camps used to be a big hospital, it was at a place called Netley, near Southampton. It had a corridor quarter of a mile long and was situated next to Southampton Water. I saw the Queen Mary pass on her way into Southampton. At this time the Suez crisis had started and this camp was an overnight stay for thousands of men that had been called up as recruits. All the vehicles were painted a light brown colour to match the sand. A friend of mine, Vic Ball from Tebay was called up, but only got half-way when he was turned back as the crisis died down.

We were cooking for one thousand men. I was getting browned off with all this moving about and taking all your kit with you, although the time seemed to go quicker. The last camp I was sent to was at Winchester. This was the training camp for the Royal Green Jackets, an infantry brigade. There were two things I liked about being there, the camp was right next to the main London to Brighton railway line and also one of the cooks there was a fireman from Rugby. His name was Ron Gilbert. So of course we were soon big mates having much in common. I was the only cook from up north out of twelve, all the others were from the Midlands and the south of England, except for the Cook Sergeant who came from Yorkshire. He seemed to take me under his wing right away, I suppose with being a northerner. His name was Arthur Craven, never to be called Arthur of course, always Sergeant, his nick name was 'Snout.' I asked the cooks who had been there some time including my mate Ron why he got this name? They said a cigarette in the army is called a snout. They were referring to the cigarette packet with the black cat on, that was going then, called 'Craven A.'

I got to like it at Winchester, so asked Snout if I could stay, this he agreed to. Anybody called Clark in the army was nicknamed, 'Nobby' and I was always given that name. As I mentioned earlier, usually anyone starting a fresh job got a trick played on him. I had only been there a few weeks, when I was grabbed with all my cookery clothes on and lifted by about six other cooks into a big tub of cold water. The tub was where we put potatoes in after they had been peeled. It stood about five foot high and measured a yard across. It didn't matter how big or heavy you were, in you had to go. I used to call it the dipping tub. I think all those lads from the south were taken aback with my accent, sometimes they could not understand me.

Not long after I was dipped, another very big lad about seventeen stone in weight came from London, his name was Alan Ebbit. He worked in the Cook House with us. I asked the lads if he had ever been in the tub? They said they didn't think so, as he was the Corporal in charge of one shift and was too heavy anyway. I told them we would have to have him dipped, Corporal or not. So this day I made arrangements to get him. I told them they would have to be willing, as he was a hell of a weight. We pounced on him, dragged him across the kitchen floor. He knew where he was going all right and put up a hell of a struggle. Finally we got him in, water flew everywhere and he had a job to get out. He was livid but knew he would have to go in once we made our minds up. Of course we had to choose a day when Snout wasn't about.

My mate Ron was a Lance Corporal and got made up to Corporal soon after I went there. So one day Snout shouted me into his office that was at the end of the kitchen, I thought Alan Ebbit had split on us about the dipping and was rather bothered. When I went in he said, "Now you are here permanent, I want to make you a Corporal as you have had a lot of experience. What do you feel about it? The pay will be a bit better and all the other lads like you." He told me what it would involve. I would be in charge of one shift, my mate Ron would be in charge of the other, early and lates. The early shift starting at 5.30am until 1.30pm and the late shift starting at 8.30am until 5.30pm. We also would have a room to our two selves, away from the other cooks. I said, "It sounds alright!" No doubt I could do the job but I was very quick tempered and if anything went wrong I might blow up. Anyway I took the chance.

There was always one cook had to stay behind for army late meals, drivers etc, usually only about twelve meals to cook and you got away about 9pm, they took it in turns. We had a butcher lad that did nothing else but chop up meat for the cookhouse, this was a steady job. We were feeding between 450–500 men. Snout always got a joint of beef for his Sunday lunch as he lived in married quarters not far from the camp, on the quiet of course. If he had been found out it would have been very serious for him, taking food away from soldiers. This day I was on late turn and got away after tea was served and after prep was done for next day. Some of the jobs the late shift lads did was to tray the bacon up, and sausage, and get all the dishes ready for breakfast. Also give the floor a good scrubbing. See to the lads that had been out on Jankers (punishment). They used to be sent to the workhouse to wash up all the dirty cookery pots and pans. Everything in there was spotless.

One lad called Alan Busby from Birmingham was the late cook on duty. I told him to put the meat into the burnell (a big oven). This he did, there were about ten large rolls of beef. The last thing I said to him was, "Now don't forget to take that meat out the burnell!" His reply was, "Ok Nobby!" When I went in the next day my mate Ron who was on early shift said, "Have you been into the back kitchen?" My reply was, "No, why?" He said, "Go and have a look." Well the meat was there on the big tray about the size of tennis balls and black as the ace of spades. Busby had forgot to take it out before he finished his shift and it had been in the oven all night. My temper got the better of me and I went up to him and called him a "Useless bugger," and gave him a nasty bat on his nose, which started bleeding. He was a lad about six foot and fourteen stone, a good mate really. Just then Snout shouted, "Corporal Clark come into my office now!" He used to stand at his office door looking over his glasses. He must have seen the carry on. Fighting among fellow mates was a serious offence in the army. I knew why I was called into his office, my brain was working overtime wondering what to say to him. All of a sudden I thought, yes, I have got one on you mister, taking the joint of beef home every weekend. Snout said, "Sit down and explain what's going on." I said, "Well I'll put it this way Sergeant there won't be any roast for you this weekend." That was it, he never said another thing to me, only I had to apologise to Busby, which I did and we were best of mates after.

Being at Winchester was a complete contrast to other places I had been at. No parades, no bulling up of kit, never wore uniform, only cook's whites, it was just like a normal job, plenty of time to yourself. One night I got washed and changed and thought I would have a walk down the town. I called in this pub called The Prince of Wales, it was on a street corner only a small pub. There were four or five playing darts and they asked if I could plays darts. I said, "A'y I can do a bit," so was asked to join them. Of course with my northern accent they wanted to know where I came from and what I was doing in Winchester. I told them I was doing National Service up at the Green Jackets Depot. One of them bought me a pint and wouldn't have one in return. He said," You will need all your money." They seemed a grand lot. From that night I went down once or twice a week to play darts and got to know the landlord and his wife. They were called Nora and Jack, a couple about sixty.

One Wednesday night I was in and the dart season had just started, as they played in a league just the same as at home. I was asked if I wanted to play for them every week, this I did. From then on, every time we had a match they would not let me buy a drink. There were six in a team and they all bought me a pint, what a wonderful crew they were. Winchester was a lovely city, with a cathedral which I had a look through one day.

Sometimes on a nice afternoon after work Ron and myself used to stand behind the cookhouse watching the trains go past, a very busy line it was. Crack trains like 'The Bournemouth Belle' came past; of course we would be talking about locos. The camp was only ten minutes walk up the hill to Winchester jail. One day Ron and myself arranged for a week-end off together, as the camp was very quiet at weekends, most of the trainees were from London and went home, so Ron went with me up to Tebay, a long way but well worth it. Once again I let him see what country life was all about, same as I did with the lad from Edinburgh. At Winchester we had about a dozen Ghurkhas attached to us, the little men from Nepal who could only speak broken English. They used to love curry so quite often we made them curry and rice, or chicken. We were told we had to look after these men, as they were rather special. The weekend Ron came to Tebay we went shooting and shot quite a few rabbits. So I gutted them then skinned them and we took them back with us to camp. We made curried rabbit for the Ghurkha soldiers, they loved it their round faces were full of smiles. I think Ron went home with me one more time before I was demobbed and we are still good friends after forty-five years. He comes to Tebay to stay now and again and my wife and I go down to his place at Rugby with his wife Veronica and son Carl.

So the days went past just doing the same thing, cooking for about 450 men, I will say this, they got a very good choice of food and very much different to me at Aldershot. For breakfast it was usually porridge or cereal, then bacon, egg, tomato, fried bread or some days sausage, it varied. Dinner was always two choices of meat and three different vegetables, plus potatoes and two choices of sweet, varying from rice pudding, sago, semolina, jam tart and custard, steamed pudding and custard. Tea was usually pie and chips or toad in the hole, sausage and chips or mash, fish or corned beef which was a fairly easy menu for us, then tea.

The time was getting close for me to be going home for good, two years had almost passed. There was a Sergeant who had a Ford Eight car just the same as I had before, he was going abroad and said I could have it cheap if I wanted it. He said I could have it for £30. I went for a ride out in it with him and it seemed to be in good order. I wrote home to dad asking him if he would lend me the money, knowing quite well he would. So I bought it, a week or two before my time was up.

On my final week Nelly and Jack at the pub gave me a farewell do, laying sandwiches on and they were all very sorry to see me go, as I was too. The night before I left Snout gave me a good handshake and said thank you for working so hard for me and I think all the boys were sorry to see me go, including Busby who burned the beef.

So I set off for home in the Ford Eight, what a way to end National Service I thought. It was a long way, over three hundred miles and no motorways then, the only time I stopped was to fill up with petrol and use the toilet, as I took some sandwiches with me and a bottle of pop, and ate them as I was driving. The little car never faltered all the way. As I said earlier, Auntie Madge and Uncle Nat Sergeant were now living at Carnforth, some twenty-five miles south of Tebay. I called in to see them and stayed the night, ready to be out of the driving seat, then carried on my journey home next day.

5

Back At Tebay

All at home were very pleased to see me back for good, grandma wasn't too well and Auntie Janie was looking after her well as she always had done. Of course the first night back home dad and I went across to the Junction Hotel for a game of dominoes, five and three's we used to play. I also saw a lot of my workmates and Nora and Jack Wharton, my mate Colin's dad and mum. Nora had been so good to me while I was away, writing now and again, sending me cuttings out of the local papers, The Westmorland Gazette and Cumberland and Westmorland Herald, if anything local was happening. My sister Marion had left school and was working in Kendal at Clark's shoe shop, no relation to our family!

In 1958 the Railway Club at Tebay was opened. It stood behind Church Street. It was called, 'The Railway Staff Association Club' and is still there today. It has seen many stars in its time, including the Nolan Sisters.

I think I had about a week off, and then started back at work on the locos. My job was waiting for me. Nothing much had changed really, only one or two had retired and left. I was back firing nearly every day now, what a difference in pay it was. My first job back at work was on early turn bank duties with Tommy Thwaites, 'Captain' as he always got called. He was always very smart in appearance; boots highly polished and never seemed to get his overalls dirty. For some reason he was badly liked among some firemen and one or two refused to work with him, but he was always grand with me. This day we had a bad engine, number 67, or small class three. It would not steam and used a lot of water, which meant having to have the injector on most of the time. The injector was a small wheel you had to turn situated in the cab above the fire hole door, this let water into the boiler from the tender. One trip we were only pushing about six wagons as the steam gauge dropped back and by the time we reached Shap summit we had to 'blow up'. This means to stand still until the steam rose again and the boiler was full of water. If the water in the boiler got very, very low, a lead plug used to burst out into the firebox,

and all the fire had to be thrown out right away. It rarely happened but was very serious when it did. I only remember on one occasion it happened to a crew at Tebay. If the water ever got that low in the boiler you should stop. You could tell how much water was in the boiler by two gauge glasses inside the cab, you could see the water level in them.

Every autumn Tebay held the annual sheep sales. These were held behind the Junction Hotel in a small field. Many sheep were sent away by rail from these sales, having sheep pens next to the warehouse on the loading bay. This day I was off duty as were a few more of my mates, so we went to the sale, not to buy any sheep of course, just for the crack in the pub. As a lot of farmers and dealers went in for a few drinks after the sale and also maybe had something to eat, I got to know some of them quite well including the auctioneer called Sam Hodgson, who lived at Crosthwaite, near Kendal. Also farmers-come-dealers, Arthur Kersey from near Penrith and Joe Rooke who farmed near Kendal. These men were also good friends of my future father-in-law, little did I know. We went into the pub at 11am and never came out until midnight having got something to eat there. The next day when I looked in my pocket I thought I must have bought a pen of sheep. The men enjoying the session with me were John Lund, Teddy Wills, Tom Greenhow, Edwin Akrigg and Jim Nicholson.

At Christmas time the landlord at the Junction ordered some beer called, 'Old Ben,' this was the real McCoy as they used to say, very strong ale and it didn't take much before you were carrying 'top weight'. The landlord's name at the time was Mick Elias. He later moved to a pub in Staveley, near Kendal. Every Christmas dart competitions were held in all the village pubs as they still do today. Up to one hundred and sixty entries took part but you were allowed two entries. The local bookmaker, called Noel Whitehead, sometimes came to the Junction and he would offer you a price either to reach the final or win it. I always had a bet on myself but never reached that far in the competition.

I was back on the road again with the Ford Eight car, and maybe had quietened down a bit, they say you always pay for your learning but I still had one or two lucky escapes. Bill Woof used to have a taxi business in Tebay. So sometimes we hired the taxi to take us to a dance if there were a few going and his daughter Vina used to drive. She married Fred

Facing page: On 24 June 1961, No 46104 arriving at Tebay on southbound express. N.E.R. line to Kirkby Stephen on righthand side with one or two wagons in N.E. yard. Of the picture on the left is the down goods yard and engine sheds.

P B Booth/N Stead Collection – John Marsh Photo Archive

Tebay Shepherds Meet behind the Cross Keys in 1940. The shepherds come to claim their lost sheep – this was held annually.

Braithwaite. We would all pile in, maybe six or seven of us. This Saturday night we went to Appleby to a dance and I was due to start work again the following morning at four o'clock. I had only about two hours sleep and had to go to work. My mate the driver was Stan Stainton, another grand chap he was. We took a ballast train to south of Low Gill on the Ingleton line. The platelayers were relaying the track, all had to be done by hand of course; a lot of the men were from Tebay so I knew them.

The train was stood still for quite a long time and we never hardly moved all morning. Stan said, "You look about buggered mate!" He didn't have to tell me, I felt shattered, having hardly any sleep being so late home from Appleby. He said, "Get curled up into that corner and have a couple of hours kip, I will look after things." This I did and felt better for it. When I woke up I was feeling hungry, so I washed the shovel off with the steam pipe and fried some bacon on it holding the shovel over the low fire. Stan said, "By that smells good, you can't beat a bit of home cured." Which it was, so I gave him a piece to taste. I said I would treat him to a pint at dinnertime after we had got relief. I wasn't really feeling like a drink of beer but managed to get one down before going home for some more sleep.

I was enjoying life to the full again both socially and work wise, fishing, shooting, hunting etc. Only been back out of the army about six months when twelve of us were told we were being made redundant. I never expected anything like that, a far worse blow than having to go to do National Service. They offered me a place at Saltly, near Birmingham and London, there was no way I was going to move, as I thought, that was the thin end of the wedge. Last in first out if I had moved. So in a month's time my life long dream that had come true, had come to an end. I finished my short career in late 1958.

Mrs Parsley, Auntie Janie, Mabel and Nora Parsley, my sister Marion at WI in 1950s.

Nat, Madge and Dad in Jersey.   *late Madge Sergeant*

6

Another Job (1958)

One day grandma's nephew from Morecambe came up to visit her, his name was Tony Whitehead and he was a builder. Tony had a relation who did all the painting, his name was Jack Townley. The plasterers were two men from Morecambe called, Brian Slinger and Alan Oliphant and a wagon fitter called Bill Cliffe. He had three drivers at that time, one of the names that came to mind was David Downey. He was a big well-built lad who lived at Heysham. Those are some of the men I remember. He had two daughters, Jean who married Archie Jackson the foreman and Brenda who had a shop in Bolton-le-Sands.

Grandma told him of my plight on the railway and he said he wanted a wagon driver, so he would take me on. I gave this a lot of thought. I was really down in the dumps, I had suffered a severe blow, but I thought well it was a job as there were no vacancies at Tebay on the railway for signal-men or Permanent Way men at the time. Tony said if I took the job he would get me some good lodgings in Morecambe, near to the Bath Hotel, his regular watering whole. He never missed a night going for a drink there. This I didn't fancy doing.

We went to visit Auntie Madge one day at Carnforth and told her the story, she said, "I could lodge with her no problem!" I thought this would be far better so I went to Carnforth to live, in late 1958, coming back to Tebay of course every weekend. There was no way I was going to lose my fishing and country life. During the week it was all bed and work, except for one night a week when I went to play darts for a pub at Holme called the Commercial Inn, with Uncle Nat. I believe the name of the pub has changed. Some of the dart players I remember were Bernard Wren, Joe Wren, Dick Fawcett and Albert Turner.

Tony was a fat man with a very rosy complexion and drove a Jaguar car, costing a lot of money in those days. The first day he came to pick me up, as he was often in Carnforth as he had a piggery there, near the canal. At the time I started, they were finishing a building site in Fulwood, Preston. So he took me down, calling at Garstang on the A6 south of

Lancaster on the way, for a cup of coffee at a small café and filling station he owned. He introduced me to the staff and told them I would be calling quite often to fill the wagon up with diesel. When we got to Preston it was about 4pm and starting to go dark. The wagon I was to drive was there loaded with all sorts of rubbish off the building site. It was a seven tonner and an old Morris. I never expected driving it that day but Tony said, "I want you to take it back to Hest Bank, near Morecambe, to a tip." I said, "Well, I haven't driven a wagon before." He said, "Git in thou'l be o'rite." Although I had driven tractors and cars this was a hell of a change. Anyway off I went quietly along the A6 through Lancaster to Hest Bank, it was black dark by then, wasn't I glad that day was over.

Tony was a man who didn't bother about anything no matter what happened, I would call him a bit of a rum bugger. He had four wagons, two of which used to carry lime up into Scotland from a quarry not far from Carnforth. They were all rough wagons and often breaking down, all painted blue. The police were never off Tony's back, for one thing or another and I could understand why.

The next job was to make a caravan park at Scarthwaite about two miles out of Lancaster on the 'Crook of Lune.' There was quite a lot of trees to fell and a hedge to pull out, so I was only driving the old wagon on odd days. We felled the trees and a timber merchant came for the trunks. We sawed the branches into logs and Tony sold them. My job was to pull the hedge and tree stumps out with a David Brown tractor and chain, then take it all away in the wagon to the tip at Hest Bank. The tip was a big piece of land that Tony owned and half of it was very boggy ground. So all the rubbish off the sites went there and was levelled out. After Scarthwaite the next building site was at Preston again, not far from his first site, down Black Bull Lane, we were going to build eighty houses. One very hard frosty morning I had to take the David Brown tractor from Scarthwaite to Preston, twenty odd miles. When I was about Garstang on the A6, the police stopped me, asked the usual questions, "Where have you come from? Where are you going? Who owns the tractor? Where is the tax disc? I got off and could hardly stand, I was frozen. I said, 'Ital' be on here likely!' But it hadn't one on! He let me go and I don't know if Tony heard any more about it.

I did the same thing at the new site at Preston, pulled the hedge out and felled a couple of trees. I used to carry everything for a house from the drains to the chimney pot with the wagon. This was another new job, so I was waiting for a trick to be played on me. This day Archie Jackson, who was Tony's son-in-law and site foreman, sent me to W.J. Cross the builder's merchants in Morecambe for some drain pipes, two tons of plaster and a drum of alcathene. This I twigged was the trick as I knew alcathene was strong pipe used for water. I was telling the man at W.J. Cross and he just laughed. I was on my way to Preston when going past the Town Hall in Lancaster, which is on a hill, I looked throught he mirror and saw a cloud of dust behind me. I knew what it was, I had lost some bags of plaster off but kept going, as I thought if the police came they would do me, so I took the chance. Again at Garstang the police surely stopped me, asked the same questions as they did with the tractor and asked to see my delivery note. Then I had to count the bags of plaster, I had lost two off. The tailboard on the old wagon came undone and they had slid underneath. I was fined two pounds a bag. Tony just laughed and said he would pay the fine. I told him that it was no good, I didn't always want the police after me. So he scrapped the old wagon and got me a brand new Austin seven tonner. What a great wagon to drive, it had a two speed axle and I carted thousands of tons of stuff in it, all to the site at Preston. Sand and gravel from Farnley's Quarry, at Carnforth; bricks from Longton Brick Works, about twelve miles from Preston; sewer and drainpipes from Darwen; small pink granite for pebble dashing from Shap Granite Works; roof tiles from Marley Tile Company in Cheshire; cement from Clitheroe Cement Works and timber and small stuff from Morecambe.

More trouble one day, I was empty and going through Bamber Bridge following this old car, I think it was a Morris Eight. All of a sudden it turned sharply to its right then turned left without giving any signal at all. I swerved to miss it but my nearside bumper and wing hit it, tipping it completely onto its roof. There was only the driver in as far as I could tell, so I stopped and went back to find an old man about seventy just lying flat on his back. When I saw he was unhurt I couldn't help but laugh to myself, it was like something you see on a film. I helped him out and he was quite OK, of course somebody had rung for the police and ambulance expecting someone to be badly hurt. I had to go to Bamber Bridge Police Station, they took details and the wagon keys off me. Told me to wait in this room while a man took the wagon for a test drive, he came back and said it was in perfect condition except for the wing been bashed in and gave me the keys back and let me go. I thought right, I will be in real trouble when I tell Tony what had happened to his new wagon. But no, he just couldn't stop laughing and said, "If I was fined he would pay for me." Luckily I never heard another thing.

My grandma Sergeant was old and pretty frail by now, and she died on 20 December 1959, aged 83 years. The wonderful woman that brought us up from that very early age had left us. She lay in the parlour (sitting room) until the day of the funeral with a bunch of her beloved Christmas Roses and a small paraffin lamp burning on a small round table beside her. They don't do that today. My brother Raymond had got married to Doreen earlier that year.

Auntie Madge looked after me like a son, but it wasn't the same as being at Roundthwaite. When I had saved some money up I sold the old Ford Eight car which had done me a great service. I bought an Austin A30 from a garage at Hest Bank, it was a very clean looking car and very good on petrol. One weekend when I was up at home a few of the lads from Tebay and myself went to a dance at Orton, only three miles up the road. I met this girl who later became my wife. They called her Dorothy Parrington, daughter of Ted and Lilian Parrington, who lived at Sim Gill Farm, at Grayrigg. We started going out together. She was one of five sisters, sadly two died. One when she was only seven, called Doreen, and Mary died aged about forty. Her other sisters are called Maureen and Peggy. Maureen lives in Burneside and is married to Ian Huck. Peggy lives at Cooper House Farm at Selside and is married to Jack Wilson.

So I was travelling home every weekend and now maybe once through the week to see Dorothy. With a stroke of luck dad said, "They wanted somebody on the Permanent Way in Grayrigg Gang." So I jumped at the job, if they would take me on. I had to go to see the Inspector who was called Bill Robinson, who was not a local man, I think he came from Lancashire. He gave me a form to fill in and made arrangements for me to have a medical, as you had to have good eyes and ears. I passed fit so got the job and told Tony I was leaving him. He was very sad about it and he said he was losing a good worker.

7

Back to Tebay Again and Retirement

I started on the Permanent Way on the 10 October 1960, the same year as Low Gill Station closed, where I had my first job. My sister Marion had got married earlier that year to Colin Chapman and was living at Winster, near Bowness-on-Windermere. So there were only dad and me left at Beckside with Auntie Janie. Little did I know at that time, that this was going to be my job for the next forty-one years.

I reported to the Permanent Way Office at Tebay one Monday morning. The office was on the northbound platform. I was given some blue overalls and a thin jacket which we called a kital, and a whistle. No high visibility clothing in those days. Jack Wharton, my mate's dad, took me to Grayrigg Station in my little Austin A30, he knew I had already had quite a bit of railway experience but this was a different job altogether. It was like starting to serve your time again. I knew the area as I had worked past Grayrigg many times on the engines. The gang consisted of five men, Tom Hayhurst the ganger, Sam Marsden, Bill Fleming, Les Taylor and me. Sam lived in a cottage about two hundred yards south of Grayrigg Station, next to the line. They were working on the track opposite his house that day. Jack introduced me to them except for the ganger who was away walking the length, which had to be done every day then. From London to Glasgow there are posts every ¼ mile situated on the downside (north bound). Our area started at Lancaster at nought milepost. Our length went from Hayfell 23 milepost in railways terms to 26½ M.P. just north of Grayrigg, five men looked after 3½ miles of track. The main tools we used for weekdays were spanners, picks, shovels, bars, hammers, jacks, rakes, scythes and hoes. It was a forty-four hour week but you were expected to work Sundays as well. We worked anywhere between Gretna and Wigan on Sundays and also on the Carlisle Settle Line. Travelling by Ribble Bus or in the back of a truck army style, if working locally we were picked up by train, usually travelling in two brake vans.

A bonus scheme had just started about six months previous to me starting and a certain amount of work had to be done each day. When we

Dorothy and me getting married at St. John's Church, Grayrigg on 24 June 1961.

Working on the line in 1963. L to R: Sam Marsden, Tom Hayhurst, Les Taylor and Colin Wharton.

were working near Sam's house, his wife, Barbara, would come out with a cup of tea for us. We had little cabins about every ¾ mile, these were made of stone or wood, with an open coal fire or a stove in, enough room to seat about six men. Some were very dark with only the doorway for light. I travelled every day in my A30 six to eight miles, having some rough trips in winter over Grayrigg Hawes, a very steep hill half way between Tebay and Grayrigg. I soon got used to the job and was enjoying it. Tom the ganger was quite strict on time, wherever we were working he would be there in the morning with the fire lit and kettle on the side. The wheelbarrow stood outside with the tools in for the days work. We had a cup of tea and sandwich around 9am, called the 'bagging'.

I saw many of my old work mates on those steam trains, I was thinking how lucky they were, on those big engines. We had to work on a Saturday morning to make our week up. The main job was oiling the points on the cross over lines and loops at Grayrigg and picking coal up for the cabins. Of course Sam and Tom hardly ever had to buy coal as they both lived next to the line, Tom lived at Lambrigg opposite the small signal box. In summer we had to mow the bank sides with a scythe, 3½ miles each side was a long way, the edges were trimmed with a hook. Then the cess weeded and raked.

One day we were working near Sam's house again when Inspector Robinson came on the scene. He was walking the track, as they had to do so much each week. Sam had quite a lot of coal dropped off the previous day, and we buried eight or nine big cobs in the ash bank. Sam reckoned it would last forever in ash, but there was also a lot of smaller bits all over the place. The inspector said in his Lancashire voice, "A see thou's started open cast mining 'aster Sam?" Sam replied in his chirpy voice, "Ay, and al tell thi' summat, am into a bloody good seam at present!"

The following year was a very busy one indeed. We were working at Docker Bridge, 23¾ M.P. doing some measured shovel packing. That meant digging the ballast out from between the wood sleepers about 15 inches either side of the rail, then after jacking the track up chippings were spread evenly under the sleeper. One man would pack while another would hand him chippings out of a barrow, onto his specially designed shovel from a canister. This was a round tin about the size of a pint pot. It was all quite technical stuff after being marked out with sighting boards and cross level. We worked to $\frac{1}{16}$ of an inch, taking slight dips out of the track mostly where the rails joined, as there was no long welded rail then. We had only been out from dinner about ½ an hour when tragedy struck the gang. Bill Fleming got knocked over by the up Royal Scot and lost his life. He was further down the track than us and no one knows to this day what really happened, although a low flying aircraft went over at the time.

This created a vacancy in the gang so I put forward my mate Colin to apply, he was working at the time for Jack Moffat and later his son, Bill, spreading lime at many farms in the area. He got the job and started in March 1961. Colin was also courting a girl from Grayrigg called Brenda Bateman, we were all very good friends and went out together. Dorothy and I were married on 24 June at St John's Church Grayrigg the same year, Colin being best man. Sam Marsden's wife Barbara made our wedding cake, she was a very good baker and made cakes for special occasions. Ted Fothergill, an ex loco mate, took our wedding photos, it was his hobby at the time. He was living at Newbiggin-in-Lune and now lives at Carnforth.

We were never still and never sat in the cabin after dinner. Always sawing wood, or looking for a good rabbit set, or fish in the beck that runs for about ½ a mile along side the railway. This day I saw two or three rabbits sitting outside their poles in the railway bank, I said to Colin I would bring the ferret next day. At dinnertime we would do a bit of ferreting if they were near where we were working. If we were staying away when dinnertime was up Tom would give us a whistle. This day the rabbits would not bolt and the whistle had gone, so we blocked all the holes up, and went early next day hoping the ferret was still there. I dug in at a hole and the ferret came out to me, probably after having a good feed and a sleep. We used to often catch some good sea trout towards the back end of the year in that beck, usually with a snare or our hands. A salmon or sea trout do some daft things. If their head is out of sight under a big stone or under the bank they think they are safe. A rabbit snare on the end of a stick, put quietly over their tail and then giving a quick tug to tighten the snare, was a good method.

This day in September the beck had dropped and the water was clear after a flood about a week previously. We were working only a few yards from the water, so at dinnertime went to look for fish. Seeing quite a few nice sea trout about three or four pound in weight, I said I would bring a snare the next day. This I did and got a long straight stick from out of a hedge. We got two lovely sea trout and hid them in long grass to be

Facing page: Derailment at Grayrigg 1966. The No 45187 was travelling to Carlisle and the driver had gone through the danger signal at Grayrigg and went into the banking. I am pictured in the middle of the picture with white arm badge and flag on 'look out' duty whilst the steam crane from Carlisle was there. Also present is 'Bate' Proctor, George Ridley and Charlie Prentice.   *Paul Allonby*

picked up later. We went about fifty yards farther up and was trying for another one when these two men approached us. It was the water bailiff and his mate. Of course out came the pen and notebook, we had been caught red handed. He took our names and addresses, also the snare and stick off us and said we would be charged. Little did they know we had two sea trout only minutes before? A week or two later came the letter, with the three charges: illegally fishing with snare and stick, trying to run away and refusing to give our names, two of which were totally untrue. We were to appear at Kendal Magistrates Court in the Town Hall. Colin would not go but I went to stand my ground on two wrong charges, which I pleaded not guilty to. We were fined, five pound each.

One frosty afternoon we were walking back to our car at Grayrigg Station around 4pm, when I saw a big tail of a big sea trout or small salmon sticking out of the bank. The water was about two feet deep but of course we could not resist having a go. Colin laid on his stomach, I held him by the ankles as the ground was on a slope, as he reached further under the bank I could not hold him and let go. Colin went in head first with a big splash. That fish escaped all right. By the time we got to Grayrigg his clothes had frozen stiff on him, luckily he had brought a change of clothing with him as he was going into Kendal straight from work. He got changed in the old Station House, which had not been occupied for some time, but he thinks to this day that I did it on purpose, as he was to be married the next day.

A house came to let at 10 Church Street in Tebay. There were fourteen houses in the street, all railway houses. Dorothy and I applied for it and were successful. This was our first home. We had little money when we were married so struggled to make ends meet. I had to work every Sunday to make a decent wage. We used to buy second hand furniture from the sales at Kendal Auction Mart. No hire purchase (borrowing) for us, we waited until we could afford it. I started doing extra jobs in the summer months such as putting wall gaps up and grave digging, in St. James' Church Yard at Tebay, which was only about one hundred yards from our house. Dorothy used to be the cleaner in the Railway Club, just across the road. The next year our first baby arrived, a son we called Raymond. For the next few years it was hard going, but we still managed a holiday, getting free travel on the railway, which was a bonus. We would often go down to Sim Gill Farm to see Dorothy's family. One day we went down and who was sat in the chair but Ernie Middleton from Davy Bank Mill,

Another view of the derailment at Grayrigg 1966. Ted Lund can just be seen on the left
Paul Allonby

Making the M6 in 1968 – notice the dust where they were blasting in the distance.

My three children taken in 1967 –
Andrew, Raymond and Angela.

he was on his rounds getting orders for provisions. He just said, "How do." I replied, then he gave a cough and said, "Dam I think I should ken thee from somewhere?" I said, "Think about Low Gill Station." His reply was, "I've got thee now, a thought a should ken thee."

The year 1962 saw the last passenger train travel from Tebay to Darlington, it was called, 'The Stainmore Ltd'. The line was then closed and taken up, part of which now is the main Tebay to Kirkby Stephen road. In 1963 our second child was born, another boy, called Andrew. The 1962–63 winter was very severe. We had thirteen weeks of severe frost every day never rising above freezing point. We were brought from our length at Grayrigg to break ice up on the Dillicar water troughs at Tebay, as were other gangs, a total of thirty men. This suited me as we got travelling time although I was living at Tebay and had not far to travel, only one mile. Some men hit the side of the trough with hammers, while others made big holes for the water to run away after a train had picked up water and it sent water flying all over the place. The line was very busy, as all the trains off the Carlisle Settle Line had been diverted via Tebay as everything was frozen up on the 'long drag'. They then went down the Low Gill branch line to join the Carlisle Settle Line at Settle Junction after having filled up with water at Tebay. We had to have a 'look out man' every day, as it was very dangerous. When a fast train went past we got down the banking and pulled our jackets over our heads as pieces of ice flew like shrapnel. It was a miracle no one got killed or badly injured. The crack express called 'The Caledonian' had just started running. This train had few stopping places between Glasgow and London and came over those troughs at around 90mph.

After about twelve weeks the snow came. It was very bad at the top of Shap summit, a goods train was stuck in a very big drift just north of the summit. We had to go to dig it out there was no chance of getting by road so they stopped an express at Tebay Station for us. When we jumped out with our shovels we were up to the waist in snow. The cutting was half full and the snow was touching the telegraph wires. After clearing the rails of snow, which took some time, the train still could not move. They put an engine on the rear as well but still no good. They then uncoupled the train in the middle and took it away in two halves. We then caught another train back to Tebay. After thirteen weeks the thaw came and it was back to Grayrigg. The track had not to be moved during frosty weather and if you got hold of a rail with bare hands it stuck to you, so gloves were always worn.

New railway bridge over the River Lune – 2 April 1983. We did all the track work and brought the line back up to standard.

1980s view of the West Coast Main Line approaching Low Gill, with the M6 Motorway in the foreground. Taken from Jeffrey's Mount on the A683 Kendal to Tebay Road.

Steve Harris

Facing page: No 85106 6M27 0631hrs at Low Gill (near the old junction to Ingleton) on 15 September 1990. These were empty tank wagons from ICI used to carry sodium carbonate from Oakleigh, (Northwich), Cheshire to Larbert, near Stirling. This was usually on Saturday mornings.

Jay Hartley

One Sunday morning we were loading rails, everything done by hand. The rails were sixty feet long and weighed a ton. It took twenty men for the job. The wagons were sixty-one feet long and we put three L-shaped irons, which fastened onto the side of the wagon – these were called hangers. The man on the end would give all the instructions – 'Get Down' 'Lift' and 'Cover.' This was a hard job for a tall man like myself if the two men either side were small men. I got my fingers caught between two rails and was taken to the Westmorland County Hospital, which was in town. Now we have a new hospital, which was built about ten years ago on the outskirts of town called the Westmorland General. I was very lucky not to lose a finger end but still have pain in it in cold weather. I was put on 'look out duties' for a few weeks. We now had another Inspector who came from Carlisle, his name was Les Mitchinson.

Tom our ganger retired and we had a farewell do in the Railway Club at Tebay for him. It was on the same day as President Kennedy in America was shot. We had a new ganger, Bob Park, he came to work in an Austin A35 van. One day we were doing some repairs at Grayrigg, a goods train went past the down line after which Bob went back onto the track. A bank engine followed it through and I shouted and whistled as hard as I could to tell him, but another train passed on the up side where I was standing blocking my view of him. I feared the worst and expected him to be dead, but by some miracle Bob was lying between the rails the engine gone over him, cutting his kital sleeve and only leaving him with a small cut on his forehead. We took him to the cabin suffering from shock and looking deathly white. He later went to hospital for a check-up.

Another lad started in our gang called, Billy Pattinson, he lived at Tebay so we took turns with our cars. He drove a Hillman Minx. Whippet racing was on the go just then. Kirkby Stephen, Penrith and Sedbergh all had a whippet club. Billy had a very good dog called Blue Haze. I think he named it after his wife, Hazel. I had one that Dorothy was not too keen on, she didn't like the shivering things. This day Colin and I were working at Hayfell and had got our job done, so would try to make a whippet trap, on the scene came Les Mitchinson the boss. I said, 'We were in for a good rollicking now.' He said in his rough voice, 'What the hell do you think you are doing?' I said, 'Trying to make a whippet trap, have you any ideas?' He smiled and gave us a hand, knowing we had got our work done.

Facing page: No's 37096 and 37072 8L65 just been loaded with ballast at Shap Quarry for re-ballasting at Clifton and Lowther, approximately five miles away. Note on the right the quarry's own trucks from which it has been loaded. Owner then was Thomas Ward. Taken at Shap summit on the 26 October 1986. *Jay Hartley*

Relaying crossovers at Lambrigg on 1 March 1987. Up line removed and re-ballasted and new track laid with concrete sleepers and long welded rails.

Jay Hartley

On the Permanent Way you could be called out at all times of day or night. One job was to guard all public crossings and bridges when the Royal Train was coming through. I remember one morning in midsummer having to go to Beck Houses Bridge, near Grayrigg. The time was 4.15am. The dawn was just breaking, it was a very warm morning, I saw a couple of thrushes rustling in the hedgerow. Then looking south I could see the glare off the fire on the Royal Train loco in the distance. The sound of the locomotive came nearer with a lovely beat. The engine on the Royal Train was nearly always a Coronation Class. It was highly polished and never had to put black smoke out, so to overcome that the fire hole door was always slightly open. The ganger had to walk his length, so long before it was due. The railway name for the Royal Train was 'Grove Special,' if the Queen was on board. If any other members of the Royal Family were travelling without the Queen it was called, 'Deep Dene.'

It was during the year of 1966 that the fish disease struck the River Lune and many other rivers as I previously mentioned. The fish broke out in big scabs and sores (U.D.N.) and all died, a disaster for us fishermen. Then the year after, they started to build the M6 motorway through the Lune Valley, which took three years to complete, the river being more like a ship canal. Muddy water with oil mixed in making fishing almost impossible.

One summer's afternoon we were working at Lambrigg right against the small signal box, at which Gilbert Holmes was on duty. He was a very good fly fisherman and a big friend of my dad's. We were having the crack with him about fishing and he said the trout would be rising about teatime, he said he would have a ride up to Tebay and show us how to catch one. We agreed to meet at 5pm at Yorkshire Bridge, near Carlingill Farm. Sure enough Gilbert was there and was just putting his rod together, when Colin and I arrived, we could see a few small trout rising. All of a sudden Gilbert clapped his hands above his head and caught a fly. 'This is what they will be taking,' he said, so got his fly box out and put a fly on matching the one he caught with his hands. The second cast in off the bridge he caught a trout which was only about six inches long but proved his point.

One day our small gang were doing some track repairs at Lambrigg. We were shovelling ballast just outside Tom Hayhurst's house when something whistled past us and landed with a big thud. It was a bullet from a .22 rifle, which had been fired across the field opposite and buried itself into the cheek of Tom's front door.

This winter's morning we were travelling to Stainforth on the Carlisle Settle line. There had been a derailment and our job was to replace the wooden sleepers that had been smashed up. We were picked up at Tebay at 3.30am with a Ribble bus. It had rained during the night then froze hard. The driver said the road was slippy and would not go down the Black Horse Hill, near Sedbergh until we got out and gritted it. The first man to get off with his shovel was Stan Cowperthwaite, a small fat man. His feet shot from under him and he went the whole of twenty-five yards on his back down the hill with his feet and arms in the air. Not a nice thing to do at about 4am on a Sunday morning. We gritted the hill from top to bottom and eventually went on our way, having a very long day not getting back home till 6.30pm.

One morning in February 1965 we were working below Grayrigg opposite Sammy's house when we saw about six men in uniform walking in line across the track coming towards us. As they got nearer we could see they were police, two had Alsatian dogs. They asked us if we had seen any one about, which we hadn't. We asked what was wrong and they were reluctant to say at first, then one of them said, 'A policeman had been shot and killed at Oxenholme Station.' I said, 'If you don't stop walking with your back to the traffic, another one of you would be killed.' They then walked on the side of the line going towards Oxenholme.

It was mostly all bed and work but I still found time for playing darts on Wednesday nights in the Shap and District League. Also the Christmas darts knockouts. There were some very good darters about including my work mate, Billy Pattinson. This particular night it was the Junction Hotel Xmas do. Jack Tallon and Ken Barnes came over from Selside. Ken was drawn against Billy, we knew this was a bit of a needle match. Billy said to him, 'If you beat me, I will eat hay with a donkey.' Sure Ken beat him and the following weekend led a donkey into the bar looking for Billy.

Our third child was born in 1967, a daughter we called Angela, but we still managed to go away for a week's holiday once a year. Our favourite place being, Butlins at Bogner Regis on the south coast. Off we would go, with three young children on the train to Euston then crossed London on the Underground to Waterloo, arriving there late afternoon.

Facing page: No 86426. 1S45 (07.50 Manchester Victoria to Glasgow and the 07.45 Liverpool Lime Street to Edinburgh) – passing through Grayrigg on 10 September 1986. These days two portions of coaches used to combine at Preston and continue as one until they reached Carstairs. The front set of coaches went to Glasgow and the rear portion to Edinburgh.

Jay Hartley

If the weather was too windy and wet, not fit to be on the track, we would play cards, Solo being the favourite game. Sam Hornby the local roadman used to call in if he saw our cars parked on the roadside and had a game with us. Tebay was a very busy place during the building of the M6. There was a large hostel (burnt to the ground just before M6 opened) at the top end of the village behind the old school. This held about a hundred men. There was also a big caravan site at Low Borrow Bridge in Mr Wilson's field. The local baker from Tebay, Glen Morgan went around every day with his van selling pies, cakes etc, he did a roaring trade. The hillside had to be blasted away through the Lune Gorge and Dorothy's mam used to take lodgers in and five or six of these men were employed blasting the hillside away. This made more work for the Permanent Way having to supply extra 'look out men' and 'hand signalmen'.

Around 1968 I was about to see the biggest change the railways had ever had. It was also about the end of Tebay as a railway village. The Locomotive Sheds closed on 1 January 1968 and the station closed on 1 July that year. Some men got jobs building the motorway while a few went onto the Permanent Way. The Railway Club was doing a roaring trade with all these M6 men and had artistes on every weekend. During 1968 I moved into a gang nearer Tebay, not as far to travel. Our length included the Dillicar water troughs where we spent all those freezing days in 1963. The motorway ran close to the track for about three miles, large dumper trucks were working day and night. One of our cabins had a flat roof. The day they opened the M6 in the autumn of 1970 we all stood on the cabin roof and waved to the first few cars that went past.

One lucky thing for Tebay after the M6 was built, they made two Service Stations, one on the west and one on the east side and a hotel only one mile to the north of the village. This has created a lot of jobs for local people. They have been voted to be the best Services in England.

More changes were to come. Diesels took over from steam, and then electric. All the signal boxes were taken down leaving only one big box at Carlisle, the next being Preston. The Carlisle box worked signals and points down as far as Burton and Holme just north of Carnforth. New signals were erected every ¾ of a mile with a phone attached, every set of points had a number on as did the signals. The power box at Carlisle is situated on the down side just south of the Citadel Station.

Facing page: No 90048 1V50 1150hrs Glasgow-Plymouth on the up line at Docker on 9 September 1990. This is a freight engine and its line distribution markings can be seen.
Jay Hartley

In 1971 there was more change for us. They did away with all the small gangs of five and made a mobile gang at Tebay consisting of ten men to look after twelve miles of track. I was the youngest man to get into it so was selected as driver, as we had a bus to travel in. Low Gill to Shap was our section. The bus had enough seating for twelve men with a small table in front of you which folded down. In the back we put all the tools in which we hung up and tied tightly, also two gas burners on which we boiled the kettle. This was our cabin on wheels as a lot of the cabins were knocked down. Our ganger was called Harvey Preston. I was on call and was called out at all times of night in all weathers, having some hectic drives up to Shap summit when the roads were bad.

My Auntie Janie had not been well for some time and passed away on 10 March 1973, aged 71. Dad was now left on his own at Beckside.

One day I was taking my old friend and workmate, Tom Richardson up to Shap, he was going patrolling. It was snowing very hard at the top and I got the bus stuck in a big drift. Before we knew the snow was halfway up the side of the bus, we never did see the railway that day. Luckily we had our dinner bags with us and plenty of water so could brew up in the bus and took no harm.

After the M6 was opened our river got back to running clear again but devoid of fish. Tebay Fishing Club introduced about twelve hundred brown trout into the river every year and still does. The time had come that we had to start and protect the salmon. So poaching and illegal fishing with rod and line was finished.

Dorothy's sister Peggy as already mentioned was now married and living at Cooper House Farm, Selside. This farm was bombed during the war, leaving only two survivors, one of which I have met. Her husband, Jack Wilson became a great friend of mine as well as brother-in-law and we often visited each other's house. Often having a drink in the Plough Inn as Jack lived only half a mile from the pub. One day we went over to see them and they had some friends from London visiting them. They came up every year and stayed near by. Jack went out to let the cows out into the yard before he milked. He noticed one was a bulling (ready for mating) so he let the bull out which was in a separate hull. The bull jumped onto the cow and did his job in seconds. The man from London

Facing page: Known either as the High Speed Train (HST) or Intercity 125. Nos 43122/104 1Z40 Derby-Gourock Charter at Docker on the down line on 1 April 1989. There was an engine at each end. These power cars were semi-permanently coupled to the coaches. These were an unusual sight up here, only used for charter, excursion or duties on the East Coast Mainline, then from 1993/4 they were in regular use.

Jay Hartley

Workers sitting on front of diesel works train just south of Grayrigg doing engineering work. The house on the right was where Sam Marsden lived.   *Jay Hartley*

All that is left today at Tebay where the busy station used to be.

John Marsh Photo Archive

had never seen anything like that before and said to Jack 'Cor blimmy that didn't take long.' Jack's reply was 'Ay we don't mess about here mate!' He took the bull back inside. The London man said to me, 'I couldn't believe it.' I replied by saying, 'what do you expect the poor old bull to do stand and lick its backside all day!' He walked away laughing and shaking his head. Jack then had started milking, wanting an early finish to go and have a few drinks with his friend up at the Plough. The breathalizer stopped our social visits to a certain extent but we still visit Cooper House.

Another big change on the Permanent Way was replacing all the wooden sleepers with concrete ones and doing away with all the jointed track and replacing it with long welded rails. These made a much smoother ride for the passengers. Our job was much the same except a lot of jobs had been done away with, mowing banks etc.

Electric heaters were fixed to points that came on automatically when the temperature fell below a certain degree. This made the job a lot easier when heavy snow fell. Another lad joined the railway, his name was Bob Kendall and he then lived at Keld, near Shap. Today he lives at Brough with his wife Margaret. One day, Inspector Les asked him why he often only came to work three days a week. Bob's reply was, 'Because I can't manage on two!' He started to learn to play the guitar and sometimes brought it to work with him to practice at dinner times and was always telling jokes. He did not stay for long on the railway. He started playing and singing Country and Western songs, is a comedian and travels far and wide and is well known for treating horses with back problems. His wife keeps horses that she rides at show jumping events and has been very successful. They are good friends of ours.

I was walking the length at Shap summit one day when I saw this man on the trackside with what I thought was a camera. As I approached him I asked him what he was doing. He said he was like a speed cop and the thing he held was a radar gun. I said to him, 'No wonder the trains can't get there on time!' He gave me a nasty look. There was a speed limit at that particular point of 80mph. People complain today of not having enough seats on trains. In the 1950s those large steam engines were pulling fifteen or sixteen carriages. Today the electrics are only pulling half the amount. I often ask myself, 'Is this progress?'

I have been called out to a few fatalities in my time, not the best of jobs. About half a mile south of Shap summit I remember a girl of about eighteen years of age was found lying beside the track, wearing only her knickers, she was minus a foot and two fingers, otherwise no other mark on her body. I don't think anyone knows to this day what had happened. I was also called out at 3am to a fatality near Grayrigg, which I don't wish to go into.

I can remember one New Year's Day, which fell on a Sunday. We were sent to work in Blea Moor Tunnel on the Carlisle Settle Line. There was a lot of snow lying and we struggled to arrive there, we were picked up by bus. Our job was to take the plates that held the rails together off and oil and examine them. The tunnel is just under 1½ miles long, we took paraffin Tilley lamps in with us, as it was black dark inside. When you could see the end it was just a pinprick of light that got bigger as you approached the end. I had been in there before so knew what to expect. When we came out this day the sun was shining very brightly on the snow and almost blinded you for a while. Sometimes people ask you silly questions, a man said to me, 'How is it that every time I go past platelayers, they are stood on side of the line doing nothing?' My reply to him was, 'How would you like to work between the rails with a train going over at 80mph?' He said, 'Oh! I never thought about that.'

After steam had finished and the M6 was now open, Tebay became a bit of a ghost village, no more sounds of steam trains whistling and chuffing and throwing clouds of black smoke out, all the shunting yards demolished, the loco sheds and station gone as well. All you can hear now is the rumble of the M6, which is left to break the silence. The bottom Co-op was made into a pub called 'The Barnaby Rudge Tavern.' The Junction Hotel closed where I had spent many happy hours and is now made into flats, but still looks the same from outside. The paddock behind it where the sheep sales were held is now built upon.

I was involved in the St. John's Ambulance for thirty years, having to pass an exam yearly. This was through the railway and we entered in many annual competitions usually held at Carlisle, and I finished as Secretary. I was also on the Committee of Tebay Football Club for a few years in the sixties. They used to run a bus to all away matches, sometimes two. They played at Keswick, Threlkeld, Coniston, Windermere, Shap, Burneside and Kendal. Sometimes the women folk would go for a couple of hours shopping. I have also been a member of the Royal British Legion for forty-five years and a member of Tebay Anglers for over fifty years.

Facing page: No. 37710 climbs towards Greenholme on 6M82, the 2025 lime empties from Margam railway yard that serviced Port Tolbot Steel Works to Hardendale Quarry on 28 May 1992. Engineering work was being carried out, down to single line working and they were travelling on the wrong line.

Jay Hartley

Picture taken by Alastair Knipe of Paul Whitehead, huntsman of the Lunesdale Pack blowing the rest of the hounds in after a day's hunting in Barbondale. *Alan Dodd*

By this time dad had been living on his own at Beckside for a long time. When he took ill and was in bed for a couple of weeks, I went across to tend to him before I went to work. Anyhow just after that there was a small terraced cottage came up for sale in Tebay, Number 2 Wood End. I persuaded him to sell up at Roundthwaite and move to Tebay. He was very reluctant to leave but he did. After a short time he went to live at Carnforth with Auntie Madge and just had Wood End for a weekend cottage and going back Monday afternoon. In 1991 he took ill and had to go into Lancaster Infirmary with a bad heart and died that year aged seventy-nine. I missed him terribly and still have my one year old birthday card signed on the back 'Love from Dad.'

About a year later another move was made altering the lengths yet again. Some Permanent Way men left and the rest went to Penrith or Oxenholme. I went to Oxenholme which was my home station. The cabin is situated exactly where the loco sheds were. There had been nothing but chop, chop with the men since 1968. This time the lengths were made longer, we were walking up to eight miles a day patrolling the track. I often walked from Oxenholme down the Branch Line to Windermere. Usually walking five miles then getting picked up at halfway. While walking past Kendal Station it reminded me of the day I was shunting all day in the 1950s. Leaves on the line seems to be a joke with the public but it isn't. One day I was sent to Windermere as a DMU (Diesel Multiple Unit) was having trouble skidding owing to leaves on the line. The woodcutters had been felling trees close to the line and, being a wet day, a lot of leaves stuck to the rails making it very slippy on the steep gradient coming out of Windermere Station. This other chap and me put sand on the rails for about three hundred yards making it easier for the trains to grip.

In February 2001 I took early retirement after serving 46½ years on the railways. During that time I have worked with hundreds of men and made many good friends. My family are all grown up and married. My eldest son, Raymond is a water bailiff on the River Eden and lives near Penruddock. Andrew is in farm work at Gaisgill, near Tebay and Angela lives on Galloper Park in Tebay. My brother Raymond became Chief Inspector at Penrith before retiring and now lives at Sandside. Doreen his wife sadly passed away this year as did Auntie Madge. My sister Marion and her husband Colin are now retired and live in Windermere.

Now that I am retired I now have more time to see and watch my grandchildren growing up. I have two grandsons, Liam and Mathew and three granddaughters, Hannah, Chloe and Jessica. I also now have more time to go hunting and fishing. The huntsman's name today is Paul Whitehead and there is nothing I like better than a walk across the fells with him. A few years ago Colin and I went to the Annual Boxing Day Hunt at Sedbergh. I decided to write a song based on that day, which I sing at the hunting social evenings, which are held at different places and have been quite successful. I'll leave you with my song, I hope you have had as much enjoyment reading this book as I have writing it.

The Boxing Day Hunt
It was on Boxing morning we went to the Hunt
We met them at Sedburgh ont Public House front
Our Huntsman, Paul Whitehead had a small glass of sherry
Then he off to the fells with his hounds in a hurry

Chorus
Tally Ho! Tally Ho!

And he off to the fells with his hounds in a hurry
Now they came round with cap just to make a few bob
Cause that fellow called Whitehead does a hell of a job
I said to my mate Colin, 'They'll get one I bet!'
And first one got up he ran right to a set

Tally Ho! Tally Ho!
And first one got up he ran right to a set

So Paul took his hounds away on a drag
They caught up with Reynard at Cautley Crag
Another fox was soon up and off like a lark
He went reet over top then through Nathet Park

Tally Ho! Tally Ho!
He went reet over top then through Nathet Park

The next time we saw him was near Fat Lamb
I said lets get to Ravenstonedale as quick as we can
The poor old fox was about tired out
And hounds away back we hallooed on with a shout

Tally Ho! Tally Ho!
And hounds away back were hallooed on with a shout.

By this time the hounds were going in full cry
Poor old Reynard was sure to die

When the hounds went past us they were going like heck
And they caught up with Reynard down by the beck

Tally Ho! Tally Ho!
And they caught up with Reynard down by the beck

So our Boxing Day Hunt it did come to a close
It was turning gay nippy I'd a drop on my nose
Ted Metcalfe and Lawrence Haygarth went home as well
Lawrence revved up his jeep and he off like hell

Tally Ho! Tally Ho!
Lawrence revved up his jeep and he off like hell.

Len

Facing page: The future – the 'Pendolino' No. 390011 - Italian made train, northbound at Lune Gorge, on a test run on 16 August 2002. The new high speed tilting train that can travel at 140mph. This is being used now between London-Manchester, London-Midland, London-West Midland; Birmingham and Wolverhampton. Then with updating of line it should be introduced later this year to Preston, Lancaster and Glasgow but keeping to a 125mph. *Jay Hartley*

If you have enjoyed this book you may also enjoy other books published by Helm Press.

'A Westmorland Shepherd' His life, poems and songs

'Elephants On The Line' Tales of a Cumbrian Railwayman (1947-95)

'Dear Mr Salvin' The story of the building of a 19th century Ulverston church

'All In A Lifetime' The story of a Dalesman as told to June Fisher

'Hawkshead Revisited" A Walk in time through Hawkshead

'A Century of Heversham and Leasgill' A walk in time through these old Westmorland villages

'An Old Westmorland Garage' The story behind Crabtree's of Kendal

'Ambleside Remembered' People and Places, Past and Present

'Snagging Turnips and Scaling Muck' The Women's Land Army in Westmorland

'The Windermere Ferry' History, Boats, Ferrymen & Passengers

'Kendal Green' A Georgian Wasteland Transformed

'Kendal Brown' The History of Kendal's Tobacco & Snuff Industry

HELM PRESS
10 Abbey Gardens, Natland, Kendal, Cumbria LA9 7SP
Tel: 015395 61321
E-mail: HelmPress@natland.freeserve.co.